You and the Broken American Healthcare System

Barbara Silliman

authorHOUSE®

AuthorHouse™
1663 Liberty Drive, Suite 200
Bloomington, IN 47403
www.authorhouse.com
Phone: 1-800-839-8640

First published by AuthorHouse 1/11/2008

ISBN: 978-1-4343-5605-5 (sc)

Library of Congress Control Number: 2007909572

Printed in the United States of America
Bloomington, Indiana

This book is printed on acid-free paper.

Dedicated to:

Jay, my husband, my lover, my best friend!
(W. Jay Silliman)

Foreword

The world breaks everyone and afterward many are strong in the broken places. (Ernest Hemingway)

You and the Broken American Healthcare System is about hope in hopelessness. We discuss America's broken healthcare system and its ravages against man and society. Then through the window of honesty, we examine the brokenness, the causes, and steps for recovery, urging community to become strong in the broken places.

We know a system is broken when it becomes antagonistic to its purpose. Healthcare's original purpose was to serve, heal, and support the injured, sick, and dying. However, facts today reveal that its purpose has changed, putting profits before healing, corporate agendas before serving, and politics before supporting.

People in a free nation, like America, have voice and collective power. Broken systems may only exist with the people's permission. Broken people permit broken systems. Therefore, to heal, we must acknowledge we have surrendered our collective power, our personal autonomies, our values, and our voices.

To become strong in the broken places, we must boldly explore all the sordid details regarding our system, mustering the strength to bear strong language, strong word pictures, and strong evidence. We must reevaluate the healthcare system that abuses and kills for power and monetary gain, knowing there is no value for life in that society.

We must question those who make profits paramount and people incidental and challenge those who make corporations king and patients insignificant, knowing there is no community in that society.

We must understand that when we give giant healthcare

conglomerates permission to monopolize resources, refuse customer service, bully, break law, and make law, we have appeased the gorillas and plundered any chance for innovative, state-of-the-art healthcare.

We must continue the march for change even when those with vested interests in the broken system mock our ideas and thwart our efforts.

We must:

• Abandon timidity

• Shun political correctness

• Speak the truth

• Become the strong, the mavericks, the changers, and the shakers, recapturing our voices, our autonomies and our power

The Broken American Healthcare System begins with the story of one man's plight, my husband's plight. Part 1: *An Upstream Family in a Downstream Society* describes Jay at the hands of this broken system and the necessary daily confrontations required in securing medical care.

Other sections of the book include Part 2: *It's All About the Money, Honey*, Part 3: *The Third Reich in America*, and Part 4: *Wake Up and Die Right*. These parts have limited information that touch only on the big issues because each could be a book within itself. There are volumes of information readily available to anyone who cares to learn more.

Many Americans have already been where Jay and I have been. We were at the mercy of a system that has no mercy - the American healthcare system.

Jay and I were a team. We met later in life, but it was as

if we had been married forever. We were cruising through life, enjoying our senior years when it hit. With no warning, with no cushions for the impact, the news blasted us! Jay was diagnosed with a glioblastoma.

A glioblastoma is one of the most aggressive brain cancers. It is mean, ugly, unrelenting, and violent. To beat this cancer for only a short time takes expertise, fortitude, and dedication at a team level.

The problem was that Jay's team only consisted of his wife, his children, other relatives, and his church family. Jay's support team was brimming with dedication, fortitude and expertise, but most of the expertise was not in medicine.

There were no doctors on our team. Throughout Jay's battle with cancer, the concept of a "medical team" was foreign to us.

Yes, Jay had an oncologist, neurologist, radiologist, endocrinologist, pulmonary specialist, and doctors of infectious diseases. However, most of them walked quickly into Jay's hospital room and quickly out of his room. They didn't turn their heads to the right or to the left. They didn't speak to Jay or to the family unless it was time for the verbal full-court-press. Their favorite place to deliver this monologue, loud and clear, was right beside Jay's bed.

Standing there, always standing there, they began to rant. Doctors declared their care was futile. They projected horrific suffering in full detail. They accused the family of living in denial. They threatened to cease care and sometimes did.

If two doctors met for Jay's benefit, the family didn't know it. If a staffing ever occurred, it took place without the most important people in the process, the patient and his support team!

After Jay's courageous battle ended, I had many questions

that demanded answers. I kept wondering why people who had dedicated their lives to healing and fighting for life could turn about-face and violate a fellow human being. How could they deny the support, the encouragement, the dignity, and the hope that the sick so desperately need? How could they refuse my husband food when he looked up into their eyes and begged for it? I began to research.

My first discovery was that doctors and hospitals receive financial incentives to expedite death rather than support life.

I learned about the politics, corruption, and camaraderie among Big Medicine, Big Pharma, Big Insurance and Big Government.

I learned about the Gestapo power of managed care. My idealistic view of American medicine quickly began to wane.

Americans have been warned for two decades that our healthcare is in crisis and headed for a major calamity. In 1996, Dr. Linda Peeno, a physician with training in internal medicine and infectious diseases, gave testimony before the United States House of Representatives. She said:

> *My work as a medical director in a hospital and as physician executive of Blue Cross/Blue Shield of Kentucky convinced me that the place made no difference. Whether it was non-profit or for-profit, whether it was health plan or hospital, I had a common task: Using my medical expertise for the financial benefit of the organization, often at great harm and potentially death, to some patients."*

Dr. Peeno testified that managed care, by nature, is unethical. She warned that the system rewards doctors for denying care rather than providing care. "It is interesting," she said, "that we speak of rationing care, and never of rationing compensation for corporation."

"We have seen during the past decade an explosion in the healthcare business," she continued, "more and more companies, executives, titles, have six-income figures." Today, in 2007, reports cite these salaries sometimes greater than Fortune 500 Executives.

According to Dr. Peeno's testimony, Blue Cross/Blue Shield paid her to restrict patient benefits even if she had to sneak in a few exclusions that patients were likely not to question. She also figured out ways to make patients' current needs coincide with prior diagnoses to establish preexisting conditions. She provided evasive information to consumers regarding their healthcare coverage, and "exploited physicians economic vulnerability" by threatening exclusion if they didn't sign on the dotted line. Dr. Peeno received lucrative financial bonuses from Blue Cross/Blue Shield for executing these maneuvers well.

Dr. Peeno left her position with Blue Cross/Blue Shield to work for the people she felt were being violated - the American consumer. "I left a six-figure job," she said, "in order to work for the persons with the least voice in health care - patients."

Consumers are the big losers in America's broken, deviant healthcare system. We are footing the bill, but we aren't in the inner circle. In addition to the Big Four, our personal dollars and insurance premiums provide the funds for doctors to form partnerships and alliances with attorneys, leaving the consumer with no recourse when abused, violated, or terminated.

After Jay's death, many attorneys admitted cause for law suit but refused to take the case citing conflict of interests due to their "social relationship" with the doctors in question.

Just as I thought I had uncovered everything, the stench became worse. I was introduced to Big Pharma's personal deception and power. I discovered their tactics through congressional testimonies, whistle blowers, and books dedicated to Big Pharma corruption. I studied Big Pharma's current medicinal ploys to rake in dollars at the expense and lives of the consumer.

Big Pharma spends an astronomical amount of money on marketing alone. Consider an estimated $12 to $15 billion in marketing to physicians and $3 billion for television and magazine articles in direct advertising to the consumer. *(Weber, 2006)*

Some doctors complain there is no money in medicine, yet build new medical clinics, drive $60,000 vehicles, and take exotic vacations. This is possible when doctors agree to take Big Pharma as their first customer, puppet corporate demands and sell drugs under the guise of consultant, educator, or speaker. This may raise the doctors' yearly incomes up to an estimated $700,000 a year.

A crucial fact in this scenario is that when Big Pharma is the doctor's first priority, the patient can only be his second. Therefore, the patient may receive the drug Big Pharma wants marketed. The prescribed drug may be new with many unknown side-effects. It may be more expensive and less effective in this situation. It may even be possible that no drug was needed or that an aspirin may have been more beneficial to the patient.

In addition to the patient being 'down the list' for the doctors' care, concern, and critical thinking, the money-bond between Big Pharma and some physicians is one reason why Americans pay up to 30% more for prescription drugs than any other country in the world.

My research continued. The medical violations became worse. I began to compare American healthcare to the Third Reich.

After reading books describing Third Reich doctors who killed and maimed instead of healed, studies that were designed to observe death rather than initiate cure, and the violation of the poor, the correlation of the American healthcare system to the Third Reich seemed uncanny to me.

Research quickly made it clear that medical abuse, killing, and negligent care is a cultural phenomenon. It is the American way. It is not a local issue. If there are still questions about national implications, the Food and Drug Administration's (FDA) documented conflict of interests, the lobbying and campaign contributions to government officials, and the involvement of America's abortionists with government, insurance, and hospitals, quickly dispels any doubt.

The facts are solid. The facts do not lie. America's health care has descended into a cesspool of deceit, exploitation, greed, and apathy, with too many under-qualified, $-focused medical staff and executives.

The facts explained it. They explained why the fourteen months that Jay and I spent 'dealing' with the American health care system were the most exasperating, tortuous, horrific of our entire lives. The very people we expected to support us, protect us, and work for us, slandered us, violated us, broke us, and on occasion tried to eliminate us.

My coin for those wrapped up in the system, those who labored to neatly groom Jay for death, is the *'qua-brutal team,'* Big Medicine, Big Pharma, Big Insurance, and Big Government!

This is where Hemingway's *"and some are strong in the broken places"* must enter into the conversation.

We still do live in a free country, fellow Americans. We still can make choices. We could turn this corruption on its head overnight!

We must reclaim our collective power, our personal autonomies, our values, and our voices. We need to unite for our own sake, our children's sake, our country's sake!

We need to focus on the angels among America's medical Gestapo. These are the ones who will lead us in becoming strong in the broken places. These angels include nurses, doctors, medical technicians, dietary personnel, rehabilitation specialists, and many others.

Many doctor alliances are forming throughout America that have become strong in the broken places. They do not yield to Big Pharma. They approach Big Insurance without fear and trepidation. They care, heal, and support.

Lee and Bob Woodruff share poignant stories about some of these doctors in their book, *In An Instant*. Bob is an ABC News Correspondent. When he was on assignment in Iraq, he was hit by a roadside bomb. The blast left him with a Glasgow Coma Scale between 3 and 4 out of a possible 15. In layman's terms, this means that Bob was neurologically almost dead.

Even though Bob was so desperately wounded, the care he received must have been awesome for his wife, Lee. Out in the middle of the Iraqi desert her husband had access to the brightest, best medical team and the most wonderful ambassadors for hope in the gravest situation.

In a television interview and in their book, they shared that if Bob had been injured in the United States, he most likely would have died. He would have died because the U.S. doctors probably would not have removed his skull to allow his brain to swell.

Lee writes, " . . .*in the middle of the Iraqi desert in some converted barracks where generators provided the power source, a surgical team that knew not to hesitate was about to cut into my husband's skull with a bone saw to relieve the rapid swelling in his brain.*"

Lee also shares that the medical team committed to Bob's care communicated with her and with one another. They brainstormed for the best possible outcome. She described the long line of medical personnel filing into the briefing room dressed in white coats, green scrubs, and military dress.

She lists the medical disciplines they represented, including trauma, surgery, anesthesiology, neurology, and many other medical specialties.

The contrast between Bob Woodruff's medical team and Jay's medical "team" is stark! Bob was treated by heroes and heroines in a desolate, foreign land, using makeshift equipment, offering hope, working diligently, waiting patiently for God's miracle.

Jay was treated by self-absorbed individuals, fighting for turf in a land of money, power, and political competition, standing by state-of-the-art equipment that they didn't want to use, constantly projecting havoc and devastation, continually ripping at Jay's soul with "I cant's and I won'ts," impatiently waiting for death and denying any chance for God's miracle.

Dr. Jerome Groopman, an oncologist and scientist at Harvard University School of Medicine wrote in his book, *Anatomy of Hope*, "A physician should never sit like a judge over a desperate patient and hand down a fixed sentence of days, weeks, or months of remaining life, even if the patient expects it.

Omniscience about life and death is not within a physician's purview."

Jay's "qua-brutal team" obviously didn't read Dr. Groopman's book or if they did, they discounted it. However, their aggression and their failure to provide a support net for us was not an end-all. Hope does not have to be given to some. Hope can be intrinsic. It is God's gift. It is a part of the resilient human spirit.

Jay and I were soul-mates; we were connected; together our eyes looked upward. We were determined to give God the last word! So we moved on. We depended on and focused on our support team. Since you will hear some of their names frequently, I will introduce them to you here.

Our family is like other families in America. We aren't perfect. Jay and I met and were married later in life. My adult children and their spouses became Jay's adopted children by his choice.

Rhonda, Delbert, Mickey, Kevin and Rose and their spouses were at our side throughout the entire horrific ordeal.

One or more of them witnessed most of the violations and conversations described between the doctors and myself. I didn't call them. I didn't ask them. They just came. Their presence and gestures demonstrated their love for Jay and me again and again.

Our church family was phenomenal. They took care of us, nurtured us, prayed for us, called us, and loved us. You will meet other supporters along the way.

At first, I thought everything in this book could be documented with hospital records or witnesses. However, after I learned that a doctor at Breech Medical Center falsified information, I knew it would take litigation with witnesses to prove what really happened. If the doctor took the time and mustered the audacity to change one record, then no record is reliable. Credibility is defunct.

I am in the same situation as Robert and Mary Schindler were when they desperately fought the system to save their daughter, Terri Schiavo. The couple and their attorney David Gibbs tried every conceivable way to maintain Terri's feeding tube. However, they were fighting a system that was equally adamant in its quest to remove the tube. The feeding tube was removed. Terri died.

In his book, "*Fighting for Dear Life,*" Attorney Gibbs states that the Schindlers were "*outgunned and out-financed.*" That is my plight. When the local attorneys told me they wouldn't take Jay's case because they were 'social buddies' with the doctors, I knew that I, too, was outgunned and out-financed. I don't have the same camaraderie, financial ties, and political cohesiveness with attorneys as the doctors do. If the doctors chose to do so, they could win the case through payoff.

So to avoid financial ruin, to avoid delay in my healing, I won't mention the names of the doctors or institutions.

It was very difficult to keep the hospitals anonymous. I really wanted to name them, thinking that notoricty would expedite their remorse and reform.

However, this book isn't about fulfilling a vendetta. It's about *YOU* – ME – all of America; I let it go!

Jay was mistreated in hospitals in three states - Kansas, Missouri, and Texas. The treatment was only minutely different from one institution to the other.

People in Colorado, Arizona, and Tennessee, vouched their healthcare was about the same. Newspaper stories from California, Georgia, New York, and more emulated our claims.

The place is incidental. It isn't just here. It's everywhere. So our thoughts shouldn't remain in Eastern Kansas. We must focus on the entire U.S.A.

My last word to you, the readers, sets my standard, explaining how I stand on things. This book is not designed to dictate your personal life and death decisions or push a political party.

The broken American healthcare system is a non-partisan problem, an *American* problem. Jay wanted the right to make decisions for his own life, and that's the same right he would have wanted for you!

Part 1:

An Upstream Family in a Downstream Society

Humility makes great men twice honorable. (Benjamin Franklin)
That's who Jay Was

The band was playing my country favorite, but I was ignoring the music to sneak looks at the man seated nearby. He drew me. Specifically, his eyes drew me with their long, curly eyelashes and look of wide-eyed innocence. The other men seemed time-worn and weathered in comparison.

I was happy to notice he was also watching me. With slow, measured movements, he approached my table and held his hand out for me. "May I have this dance?" he asked.

We danced. We chatted. We laughed, ignoring the change partner signals. We two-stepped to the oldies and we glided through the contemporaries.

Then when the evening was over, Jay said simply and sweetly, "I have waited ten years for you. Can we see each other again?"

We became inseparable -- inseparable in spirit, because we actually lived several hundred miles apart. Jay worked for the Kansas Department of Transportation, KDOT, and I was a paraprofessional in a local school district. In spite of the distance between us, Jay became my rock. He was supportive and loving, and he never asked for anything in return.

We weren't "*spring chickens*" when we met. Jay was sixty-three and I was forty-nine. My age was guessable, but Jay didn't look sixty-three and he didn't act sixty-three. Both his parents lived close to the century mark and we believed Jay was destined for the same.

One year later, Jay and I were married in a little Baptist Church in Hays, Kansas. It was a simple, family-style wedding.

I preferred to be married by a minister in private; Jay wanted to be married in a small church wedding. So we invited family,

Barbara Silliman

exchanged the vows we had written for each other, and became true soul-mates under God in that ceremony.

Jay was a farmer with a talent for doing a little bit of everything. He worked on machinery. He climbed on the roof to fix shingles. He helped me refurbish our home in Topeka, Kansas, putting in sinks, garbage disposals, and rugs.

He was a model of working dichotomies. He was slow moving, yet timely; methodical, yet flexible; casual, yet focused. When I came up with a new or unusual project, he good-naturedly joined the ranks.

One day when I was cleaning the bathroom, I saw an edge of the wall paper had come loose. "I really don't like this paper," I thought. So I grabbed the edge and pulled hard. A huge piece stripped off the wall.

I walked into the living room where Jay was reading, held up the piece of wallpaper and said, "You want to help me wallpaper the bathroom?"

He looked up from his book. He quickly moved his eyes to the wallpaper hanging from my hand. Then he looked back at me. His eyes were wide in amazement, but he spoke in his usual slow, John Wayne style, "That might be a good idea," he said looking at the wallpaper in my hand again, "if the wallpaper is no longer on the wall, but in your hand."

Even though I consistently surprised Jay with my spontaneity, my call for help in the middle of projects "gone bad" and the request for sudden wood-work gift specials, he never raised his voice or reprimanded me. He just always pulled me through.

Jay could do this. He accepted people for who they were. In fact, that was his motto. When I would come home and gripe about this person or that person. Jay would kindly, softly state, "Just let them be who they are."

Since I am a type A, highly opinionated person, Jay may have said this to me a few hundred times in our life together. He always gave others the benefit of the doubt, many times saying: "A person can only do what he knows to do."

Jay never protected himself. He never advocated for himself. He took life's blows and worked a little harder when things went sour. However, he did have a line that could be crossed. He called them "deal-breakers," springing into action if the issue threatened my safety, my wants, or my needs.

That's who Jay was.

Jay and I loved garage sales. Our home was almost entirely decorated in used décor. I guess we were fairly good at it because people told us our home was beautiful. I credit this to Jay for he had a special gift for seeing unusual, charming pieces.

One afternoon as Jay and I were hitting all the prime garage sale spots, I looked down at the gas gauge and saw it was getting close to empty. I said something about needing to buy gas.

Jay looked at the gauge and said, "You have enough to get home. Why don't we wait and buy it when we get to the North side of town? It's cheaper there."

I agreed and we continued our shopping spree.

The next day was Sunday. Jay and I always went to church together, but this morning Jay was going to stay home to get things ready for a trip. We needed to leave on our trip before noon. So the plan was that I would teach my children's Sunday school class and come home before church. I got up, dressed, and started out the door.

"Oh, my goodness," I said. "I had better hurry. I forgot to put gas in the car when we came home last evening. I have to get gas before I can go to church."

I kissed Jay, grabbed my Bible, and dashed out the door. I drove to the gas station about five blocks from our home. I pulled up to the gas tank and started to walk around the car when I saw him.

There was Jay, in all his merciful, giving nature, getting out of his pickup. "What are you doing here?" I quizzed.

"I thought I left you at home."

"It's my fault that we didn't get gas yesterday," he said. "I didn't want you to put gas in the car in your good clothes." He filled my car with gas.

I walked up to him, kissed him on the cheek, looked into those soft, sweet eyes, and said, "You never cease to amaze me! I love you so much. Thank you."

That's who Jay was.

When my Dad was ill, it was encouraging to watch him

respond to Jay's kindness. A visible transformation took place when Jay came near. Dad was a good man, but he was not the gentle soul that Jay was, swearing that "double-talk, patronizing, and insincerity were his pet peeves."

Since Jay was patient, since he was never pushy, since he had an intrinsic nature to help without offending, Dad judged his motives pure. He saw Jay as genuine, a man with no guile. So unabashedly, he accepted Jay's touch, encouragement, and help.

Jay and I went to Kentucky when my brother was dying of diabetes, visiting him in the hospital. My brother tried to turn in bed and moaned. Then in a strained whisper, he said, "I'm thirsty."

Several people were in the room, including my brother's wife and myself. However, it was Jay who reached for the water cup. It was Jay who held my brother's head to give him this moist moment of peace. It was Jay who helped him reposition himself in bed for comfort.

That's who Jay was.

When Jay and I visited relatives in Colorado, they reminisced about the good old days. One neighbor described Jay in the early years:

"Day after day, Jay farmed without help," he said. "In wheat harvest he would cut a load of wheat, take it to town, come home and cut another load of wheat. He was slow, quiet, methodical and efficient."

"Uncle Jay and Uncle Bill were wonderful to Mom and us six kids when dad died of a brain tumor," Doris, Jay's niece bragged. "Mom's two brothers stepped up to the plate. I don't think we could have made it without them."

"I have asthma," Jay's daughter shared. "I used to beg Dad to take me with him to grind grain for the cows. He wouldn't let me go with him, but he would bring me a little bucket of grain and say: "'you can grind your grain while I am grinding the cow's grain. I will be back soon and we can do other things together." '

That's who Jay was.

The Toy Story, Nemo, or any other G-rated animated delights were the highlight of our social life. Sometimes we took our grandchildren. Sometimes we sneaked in alone. You can call it 'old people crashing the babies' party' or you can call it 'two past-fifty folks who never grew up'!

We yearned for the idealistic innocence portrayed in yesterday's films. These animated features filled the bill. So we jumped in our little hot-rod and raced to the theater.

When Jay and I first began dating, someone ask my youngest son, Kevin, what he thought of it. "How could I dislike someone who made my mother laugh again?" he asked.

Shela and Anne, two adopted daughters-in-law, vowed they wouldn't only take care of Jay if something happened to Mom first, but they would fight over him.

Now that is true testimony to who Jay was.

Calamity Hits

You can't know how you would behave in a crisis until it drops out of the sky and knocks you down like a bandit; stealing your future, robbing you of your dreams, and mocking anything that resembles certainty." (Lee and Bob Woodruff, 2007)

When Jay began to have the first symptoms of the cancer that would kill him, I missed all the signs. Today, I look back and am appalled at what I didn't see.

There were never any headaches. There were no seizures. His personality didn't change. But there were subtle indications.

The first two things I noticed, without noticing, was that Jay occasionally jumped the curb when he turned onto another street, and he waited for cars far in the distance before pulling out onto the road in front of our driveway.

These incidences should have jolted me! After the tumor was diagnosed, I scolded myself. "Those were signs." I said. "They were literally slapping me on the side of my head! And I didn't see them?"

Jay worked for KDOT. He was adept at driving large equipment and machinery. He had a chauffeur's license. He was an excellent driver, but I didn't question why he suddenly jumped curbs?

In retrospect, I realize Jay also was losing some of his mechanical sense. However, at the time, I had reasons to explain everything. He had trouble setting the home alarm system. I blamed the system. He was doing less handiwork around the house. I thought he deserved a rest. He complained he had botched this job or that job on the farm. I thought he was being too hard on himself.

Jay also had three accidents in close proximity. The first calamity was a sliver of steel in his eye. He said he didn't use goggles because the grinder had a shield on it. I remember remarking, "Obviously, not a good enough shield. Please be careful. I love you."

I was concerned, but thought about all the dangerous jobs Jay did every day. I rationalized that it was a wonder he didn't get hurt more often.

Next, Jay hurt his leg. He told me a calf pinned him up against the fence when they were working cattle. After an x-ray, we learned that he had cracked a bone in his leg and he had to wear a brace for awhile. That didn't seem unusual either. This type mishap isn't uncommon on a farm.

Later, Jay cut his hand while using the home table saw. "You've never had safety training for using this equipment," I said. "It has always worried me when you used the table saw." I was thankful the cut wasn't worse than it was.

Other things happened and many were strange or unusual. However, Jay never complained. He didn't say he hurt anywhere. He didn't have a fever. He continued working, eating, visiting.

Jay began to search for foul smells. I would help him look, but I couldn't smell it myself. I thought it might be a mouse smell so I searched for a dead mouse. I thought it could be my breath, so I brushed both my teeth and my tongue and gargled mouth wash. I double-checked the laundry basket. However, once we were satisfied the smell was gone, we would forget it until the next time.

Later, I began to notice that one or two of the plastic pieces on the Venetian blinds in the bathroom and dining room were bent back. A couple in the dining room had actually been bent off so there was a little peek-hole you could look out.

I thought maybe one of the grandkids was doing it so I said, "Jay, there are some broken places in the Venetian blinds. Do you know who could be doing that?"

"Yes," he said. "I'm doing it."

"You are," I exclaimed! "Why are you doing that?"

"To see out," he answered.

Puzzled, I said, "It would be better if you lifted the plastic piece rather than break it off."

Even though this seemed really out of character for Jay, I didn't question him any further. Everything must have been working on me subconsciously, however, because I desperately wanted Jay to quit the farm. I didn't want to demand he quit. I wanted it to be his choice.

So I decided to open a little second-hand furniture store, thinking his love for garage sales would make him want to be a part of it. It seemed to work. He quit the farm to work in the store.

However, looking back now, I think he was worried about finances and chose to work in the store rather than hire help.

Jay worked in the store for a few months and then the crises suddenly erupted! He began sharing daily store information with me. However, he would either begin talking in the middle of a sentence and I would say, "Now what are we talking about . . . . ?" Or he would stop right in the middle of a sentence and I would question, "And . . . and . . . and?"

I explained what he was doing and asked him if he knew it. He said, "Yes, I know I'm doing it, but I don't know how to stop."

Concerned that he may have had a mini stroke, I immediately called the doctor. He ordered an MRI, Magnetic Resonance Imaging.

Within a couple of hours after Jay went in for the MRI, the doctor called us and ask us to come to the office. I wasn't frightened or upset. I thought the doctor would say it was a mini-stroke and Jay would be okay in a couple of weeks.

"We did find something on the brain," the doctor said. "However, it isn't a mini-stroke. I can't tell you for sure, but it is most likely cancer. I'll take a chest x-ray here and refer you to an oncologist. Who do you want me to call?"

Jay began to cry. "I have cancer," he said.

I couldn't believe it. It felt as if the doctor had swung a baseball bat into my diaphragm. I couldn't breathe. My skin went cold.

I didn't want to talk. I didn't want to respond. I wanted to wake up.

However, I knew Jay couldn't talk. He wouldn't talk. He was a thinker, not a talker. He never engaged in conversation with others about things he didn't understand. So I stepped in, as usual.

"We don't know any oncologists," I blurted. "So I can't tell you *who* we want, but I can tell you *what* we want. Please refer us to someone who is brilliant.

We want him to be on the razor-edge in his field. He needs to be a maverick, a trailblazer, someone who will challenge the status-quo. Please!"

Unrelated thoughts flooded my head, maybe to protect, maybe to diverge. I thought of a conversation that Jay's sister and I had weeks earlier. "Barbara," she said. "Even though you are several years younger than Jay, have you ever thought that you might die before he does?"

"Certainly," I said. "If you consider your family tree and my family tree, we'll 'check out' at about the same time. My family only lives to their early eighties. Your family lives into their middle or late nineties. Do the math. It says it all." Then we laughed.

That conversation was no longer funny. The idea that we would "check out" at the same time was always prevalent in my mind. This pre-conceived notion about going hand-in-hand into eternity may be one reason why I couldn't see the warning signals flashing before me.

Angels Among Us

We seldom look beyond when we are in the trenches raising our children. But one day we sit up and take notice: They have grown up and are now the giving, special people we hoped they would become. The physical care has reversed; the mature love has encircled. (Silliman, 2007)

Jay and I were overwhelmed with a disease. We were overwhelmed with strategies for care. We were overwhelmed with a store full of quality second-hand furniture and décor. The site landlord suggested having a huge sale.

However, a huge sale was not an option for us. Our energy was spent; our business sense was exhausted; our stamina was depleted. We knew that re-pricing merchandise, smiling through days of busy sales, boxing the unsold merchandise and cleaning the premises after the sell-out was not in Jay's best interest or mine.

Jay and I had developed a friendship with the owner of *Second Time Around Furniture Store* in Hays, Kansas. When I called her, she agreed to take everything in our store on consignment. What a relief!

Church family inventoried the store merchandise, and boxed each item for the trip, carefully wrapping each piece of China, each delicate ceramic, each crystal candle holder.

Delbert rounded up the grandsons from school, college, and work and headed for Topeka. Jay and I sat and watched as they began to load the merchandise into the trucks. They worked in amazing streamline precision.

Each man was in the right place at the right time. They looked as if this was an everyday business practice, even though it was their first time. Someone grabbed a chair, a box, or a bed and relayed it to the next man in line.

Without fanfare, without ado, he tossed it on to the man at truck-side who secured it in place for the ride.

They finished the job in record time – one short afternoon.

As the trucks sped down the highway, Jay and I were free to take care of the pressing matters ahead of us, his decisions, his care, and his future.

The Man of No Words

Competency is not separable from communication skills. It's not a tradeoff. (Judy Hall, Social Psychologist)

We met with the first oncologist assigned to us. We felt he was cold, distant. His eyes were intense, probing us without words, without expressed meaning. His spoken words were few and guarded, and he engaged in real conversation only when I became too animated for his temperament or questioned him unceasingly.

The oncologist rapped Jay on the knees and looked into his eyes, but didn't try to engage him in conversation. He sat there and stared at Jay in silence. Later we wondered: "Did he think Jay wasn't there? Did he think Jay's mind had already been swallowed by the thief inside?"

Since Jay wouldn't speak to the doctor without encouragement, I again became the orator for the day: "What do you think we are dealing with here?" I asked.

"We don't know," the doctor said. "It depends on what the tests show. We'll do a CT Scan (Cat Scan) to see if there are any cancerous lesions anywhere else in the body."

"Do we hope we find cancer? Will there be a better chance for cure if it's a secondary cancer or if it's a primary brain cancer," I quizzed.

"It depends on what it is," he replied. "I can't tell you that."

"Whatever it is, Doctor, please listen to our wishes. Not treating is not an option for us no matter what it is! We want you to think of Jay as you would think of Lance Armstrong. Go for the gold! If for some reason, Jay's age, the cancer type, or your personal beliefs will prevent you from treating Jay with state-of-the-art procedures, please refer us to another oncologist."

After making no comment and staring at me with those penetrating eyes, he said, "Will you be home tonight?"

"We'll be where you want us to be, when you want us to be there. You just name the place and the hour," I said.

"Okay," he said. "I'll call you tonight with the CT results." Then he added, "I'll call either tonight or tomorrow."

As we left the office, I felt very uneasy. The man was so unemotional that he seemed a million miles away. For some reason, I felt he could have diagnosed Jay's condition within 99% accuracy at that moment and he could have given us triple the amount of information. "That 'guy' had about as much energy as a snail climbing up the side of the fish bowl," I told Jay.

"Oh, well," I said half under my breath. "He said he'd call us tonight or tomorrow. Tomorrow is Saturday. If he'll call us on a weekend, that's something."

We waited. Jay sat in his recliner and I sat in mine. We didn't want to watch television. We didn't want to eat. At times, we cried. At times, we just held each other in silence. Most of the time, we prayed. Finally, we conceded that the call wouldn't come tonight. We went to bed uninformed and waiting.

The next morning we lay in bed for awhile, holding each other. Everything was surreal. It was as if we were there, but we weren't there. I began to worry.

Maybe Jay was so full of cancer the doctor didn't want to call and give us the bad news on a weekend. Jay kept saying, "They are wrong. I'm okay."

We waited through Saturday. No call. Sunday we pulled ourselves out of bed and went to church. Then we came home and sat in our recliners again, going through the same ritual. We didn't feel like eating; we didn't feel like watching television.

Sunday night I asked Jay if he wanted to call any of the relatives. "I don't think so," he said. "Maybe we should wait to see what it is first."

"If we call Kevin, Jay, he will pray with us," I softly suggested.

"Okay," he said. "Let's do call him."

After we went to bed that night, we called Kevin from the telephone on our night stand. He prayed with us.

Then he said, "I love you, Jay. Did our prayers make you feel better?"

"Yes," Jay said through his tears. "But it made me cry."

"Hey, man, it made me cry too. We love you. Hang in there, ol' buddy."

Then we cried together.

The same desperation, the same waiting continued on Monday. Morning came and went. There was no call. At noon, I called the doctor's office. "The doctor is out to lunch," the nurse told me, "I'll have him call you when he returns."

We waited. In the late afternoon right before closing time, I called the doctor's office again. This time I spoke to an answering machine. I identified myself, gave my telephone number, and left a curt message, "You did say the doctor would call me upon his return to the office! Is he back from dinner yet?"

The doctor called with no apology, no excuse, and no overt signs that anything was amiss. He simply said that Jay's body was clean. The CT scan didn't reveal any cancer.

Whatever was in Jay's brain was our culprit. The oncologist referred Jay to a neurologist.

Sanity Overruled

The most wondrous technology exists that can pinpoint the exact location of a tumor, thread a tiny catheter up into the brain to open a clogged artery, pulverize a kidney stone without breaking the skin. But the simple stuff - like getting an MRI on time, being given the right drugs at the right time, making sure everyone knows which side of your brain to operate on - can cause the biggest problems. (Gibbs and Bower, 2006)

The neurologist scheduled Jay for a brain biopsy at the end of the week and told us that Jay must go to the hospital the day before surgery for an admittance examination.

We arrived at Breech Medical Center early that morning. The reality of the situation was frightening. We felt stranded among strangers. Most of the personnel we spoke with seemed to have no people skills and the ones who did were so cramped for time, they couldn't demonstrate them.

Our family doctor was unavailable at this point. He didn't have hospital privileges. "Oh, well," I assured Jay, "He just addresses the easy issues like the common cold or the flu anyway. He's basically a broker for all the specialists in the city."

I didn't share the reality of our plight with Jay, but I knew the hospitalists were our only recourse. And I knew that was not going to be good!

A hospitalist provides medical care for patients in a hospital setting. The patients have personal physicians, but their doctors can't see them in the hospital for various reasons. They may not have hospital privileges or they may need assistance due to patient over-load or conflicting medical responsibilities.

A patient may see several hospitalists during one short hospital stay. It is difficult to develop a relationship with any of them in this limited time.

Also, hospitalists are free to give their opinions. So a patient may hear multiple stories regarding his condition, depending upon the hospitalist medical focus or world views.

Jay received an ultra sound on his carotid arteries. He took blood tests. He went through the battery of do's and don'ts before surgery. When he received his okay, we went home to return early the next morning for a brain biopsy.

However, during the evening hours, the telephone rang. "Hello," the voice said, "I am a hospitalist at Breech Medical Center. I am calling to tell you that we can't do the brain biopsy tomorrow after all. The sonogram of your husband's carotid artery indicates blockage. If the artery is blocked as the sonogram indicates, your husband could have a massive stroke or die on the operating table. Sometimes the sonogram is inaccurate, however. So we need to do an arteriogram to validate the condition of his arteries."

"Please come to the hospital at the same time you were scheduled tomorrow," he continued. "We will do the arteriogram rather than the brain biopsy at that time. I'll be there so everyone is on the same page and everything will run smoothly. See you then."

The next morning we arrived at the hospital. There was complete bedlam. No hospitalist was around and no one knew where to take Jay. Everyone was talking at once. No one seemed aware of the patient.

Staff was talking to staff, staff was talking on the telephone, staff was questioning those who walked near the reception desk, but no one was talking to Jay. One nurse said. "The neurosurgeon doesn't know the procedure has been postponed."

Voices were talking, questioning, "Shouldn't we contact the neurosurgeon?" . . . "Where shall we put the patient?"

Other voices chimed-in saying let's do this or let's do that. Then a voice rang above the rest, "Well, how about pre-op? That's where I'd take him."

So they began to walk Jay in that direction. I was getting really, really nervous. My body was in flight or fight mode. I knew if a gurney came to take Jay for the brain biopsy that I would personally tackle it!

They weren't going to cause my husband to have a massive stroke because they didn't know what they were doing.

When we arrived in pre-op, the bedlam continued. Again no one knew what to do with the patient. Jay was crying and I began to cry. "The last place I want to be where they don't know what they're doing," I said with slow, emphasized, spaced wording, *"is- - in - - the- - hospital!"*

Someone called the clergy without my permission and he joined the utter chaos telling me, "Well, if you don't think you have done something, you have. It's not everyone who has an appointment with an oncologist, neurologist, radiologist, and a brain biopsy scheduled in a week."

His voice blended with all the other sounds in the room and I was wondering, "And what good does expediency do when at the crucial time staff is clueless. Absolutely no one knows what he or she is doing."

I kept begging God for the military medical team I had heard about on television:

A news report said that in the Iraq war 96% of the injured soldiers who make it to the battlefield medical centers are saved.

The reporter asked a nurse, "How is this possible? These medic centers are crude. You use generators for electricity. The men and women brought to the centers have horrible brain and other injuries!"

The nurse simply answered, "We all know our jobs and we do them!"

A person dressed in a white coat, wearing a facial mask walked into the room. He looked at me and barked, "What do you want us to do?"

I barked back, "I want you to do what you are supposed to do! And I want you to *know what that is!*"

He turned on a pivot and briskly left the room. I recognized the next face in a white coat. It was Jay's neurosurgeon. He said they would be taking Jay for the arteriogram within the next few minutes.

Later, in the cafeteria, the nurses in pre-op came over to my table and hugged me. They said that the scene in pre-op was detestable and apologized for the uproar. They also told me that they took Jay for his arteriogram early because of the mix-up. He was scheduled for afternoon, but after the *"no one knows anything"* scene, they took him immediately.

Jay and I were quickly getting an education. At this most crucial time in our lives, we were finding that our doctors weren't dependable. They didn't carry through. Their words had no meaning. It was frightening. We were injured people on a shaky bridge. We were looking for pillars of strength to embrace us. There were none in sight!

Angels Among Us

The joy in sorrow, the peace in tragedy, the light in darkness is the sweet, sweet hand of Jesus touching you through the family he has given you. (Silliman, 2007)

Each individual is gifted, and each contributed in his or her own unique way. Jay knew it. He felt it. He voiced it.

Delbert and his family cleaned out the store. He also brought his golf cart so Jay and I had a way to drive over the back lawn from the lower back door to the front door.

Rhonda and Jay had a special friendship. In conversation or in silence, they understood each other; the dynamic of brother/sisterhood was always there. Rhonda's history in the medical institution and her social service expertise were invaluable to us.

Mickey, Anne and family had a close relationship with Jay. He loved to see them come and hated to see them leave. Mickey was our 'money' man, helping me juggle funds to get us where we needed to go, buy the things we needed to buy, and pay the bills when they came due. He also helped us with mechanical repairs.

Kevin and Shela were with us through many hospital crises. They stood beside us, supported us, and nurtured us. Kevin hugged Jay and prayed with him often. Shela boldly stepped forward, directing, when the hospitals forgot their calling.

Rose, Don and family helped daily. They relocated to be beside us. They cleaned, vacuumed, and dusted. They read to Jay, watched videos with him, and helped him put puzzles together. Don changed light switches, installed needed equipment, built a ramp and safety apparatus. He picked Jay up and carried him on more than one occasion.

Murdering Hope

For all my patients, hope, true hope, has proved as important as any medication I might prescribe or any procedure I might perform. (Groopman, 2004)

Jay was readmitted to Breech Medical Center to undergo a brain biopsy. Both Rhonda and Kevin left their jobs and families to come and support us. Their support was our sole source of strength outside our faith. Many of the nurses were kind, but they were overscheduled and overworked. The neurosurgeon didn't come see us or reassure us. He didn't talk to me before the procedure, and he didn't visit with Jay either. We were just there; no one prepared us for anything.

When Jay was situated in his room, the nurse entered and started a Dylantin intravenous drip.

"Why are you giving Jay this medication?" I asked.

"It's to prevent seizures," she said matter-of-factly.

"Why are they giving him seizure medication when he has never had a seizure," I questioned.

She simply replied, "It's doctor's orders."

I was perplexed. Medicine is not my forte. I've never been trained in any medical procedure, I have had no medical experience, and I would never have chosen medicine for my professional career. Since I was completely new at this, I had no clue what was happening. I needed some conversation!

Suddenly, Jay's eyes began to roll back into his head. The color drained from his skin and lips. He moaned and stretched out 'spread eagle' across the bed, grabbing at the sheet with his hands. He looked like he was trying to break a long distance fall.

"What are they doing to me," he cried.

I freaked. I thought I was losing him. I ran to the nurses' station and tried to steal someone, anyone, from their stories and laughter. I must have looked somewhat like Paul Revere, waving my hands and dancing around, but I felt invisible because no one responded to me. It seemed like they were looking right through me. I couldn't stand still and I couldn't wait. I ran back to Jay's room crying.

Then Shela checked Jay's blood pressure. She briskly marched out to the nurses' station in a controlled, professional manner and commanded, "Excuse me! Jay needs a blood pressure monitor stat. His blood pressure is falling rapidly!"

The authority in Shela's voice was apparent. The nurses looked up. They sensed her expertise and knew she was one of them. They immediately stopped laughing and ran into Jay's room to help stabilize him.

The Dylantin had already yielded its punch. Jay was delirious, talking out of his head in unrelated sentences. I complained. "Dylantin doesn't make people delirious," the nurses said in defense. "It's most likely the tumor."

The family all looked at one another with raised eyebrows. We knew better than that. We all saw it happen right before our eyes! Feeling our frustration, the nurse told me that I needed to visit with the pharmacist about the Dylantin. She called and asked him to come visit with me.

The pharmacist was soft-spoken, kind, and helpful. "Jay probably is receiving Dylantin because he is scheduled for a brain biopsy. The biopsy can cause seizures. Dylantin will help reduce the chance for seizures during and after the procedure."

Then his eyes met mine. Sincerely, compassionately he assured me, "You have the right to ask questions and you *should* be asking them," he said. "The doctor *should* have visited with you about this way before now."

However, no doctor, up to this point, had even tried to engage Jay in conversation, and they were beginning to avoid me at every opportunity.

Jay summed it up in one simple statement, "They think I'm dead already."

If the apathy, non-care, and ill-treatment had been sporadic, intermittent, we might have said it was due to individual deficiencies. However, the emotional battering felt constant and the attitude typical of most health care staff we met.

It was as if their behaviors were structured, programmed, mandated, protocol for the terminally ill. Jay and I called it the 'DOA Factor' (Dead-On-Arrival). We also agreed that white-coats who deem a patient DOA when he is a living, breathing, relating, human being are attempting to kill him in the same manner as the thug on the street shoots a man in the back.

The brain biopsy came back Glioblastoma Mediforme Stage 4. This diagnosis meant that Jay had one of the most, if not the most, aggressive malignant brain tumors. There were so many tragedies in this diagnosis. We suddenly knew that everything we had endured to this point was minor in comparison to what we were about to face.

Once the diagnosis was announced, the oxymorons, euphuisms, hype, half-truths, lies and marketing began in earnest. Negativism was the order of the day. They would stand beside Jay's bed and monologue about what he was going to face.

"*He is seventy-eight years old.* There's nothing we can do. We have never beaten this type of cancer. *Don't go to Cancer Centers of America.* Jay won't be the first to conquer this disease. *He is seventy-eight years old.* Jay will be dead in two months. For his sake, you don't want to prolong his life. We doctors must honor the Hippocratic Oath and first do no harm. *Don't go to Cancer Centers of America.* His heart won't last through treatment. He has an abdominal aneurysm that could burst in treatment. *He is seventy-eight years old.* Older people die quicker with this cancer than younger people. *Don't go to Cancer Centers of America.*"

Not one doctor, not one nurse, not one medical staff told us that they would support us in our decision to fight the cancer. Not one word was said about places in the country that are on the razor-edge in the fight against the glioblastoma. No one told us Duke University in North Carolina was helping patients with brain tumors live for five years or more.

No one explained that when all else failed, they could give Jay an experimental drug. No one talked about available mercy flights to transfer patients to a more informed medical institution.

Above all, no one began to educate me to care for Jay. When I asked the doctor what I could do at home or if I could provide nutritional support in some way, he condescendingly barked, "No, diet ever cured cancer!"

A cruel, demented king in ancient times, Etruscan King Mezeatius, tied his captives to decomposing corpses as punishment. The stench and the weight of the body dragged the prisoners into the depths of despair.

Our experience was like that. It was as if the doctors, nurses, and healthcare staff were demented. Like King Mezeatius, it seemed they made every effort to tie Jay to "death" itself.

A few mentioned death kindly, as if it were Jay's long, lost friend. Some focused on death's lightning speed and final devastating blow.

However, most of them lingered. They lingered on death's pathway, the hurdles, obstacles, and painful thorny patches awaiting us. This lingering majority were obsessed. They were obsessed with gory details, demonstrating an attempt, or ignorance, for strapping Jay to the futility of his situation and tying him to his own corpse before he died.

Angels Among Us

Doctors hold the world in place for patients. We establish the legitimacy of their claims. We offer human contact and concern apart from the private contest of sympathy. (Stein, 2007)

It may seem strange to some women to see their husbands cry. However, Jay acknowledged his emotions. He and I cried together many times, showing feelings of sorrow, compassion, and joy. Tears weren't a sign of weakness for Jay. He was secure in his manhood and crying was just a part of life.

Jay didn't cry at home anymore than he ever did, and his tears in the hospital were always connected to a reason. He cried every time he thought someone was treating me with disrespect. He hated to hear someone argue with me. He said, "I don't like it when they talk to you like that. It frightens me because I can't protect you."

"Don't worry, Jay," I said. "I'm a tough old lady and I'm fighting for my best friend. I'm fighting for the man I love. Hang in there, Sweetheart. We will prevail!"

One day an 'Angel' came by our room. She was dressed in white, but had no visible wings. You knew she was an Angel, though, because she said, "If Jay is uncomfortable, if he needs your embrace, that hospital bed is big enough for both of you."

I climbed into the hospital bed beside him. I wrapped my arms tightly around him, and whispered "I love you" over and over in his ears. After that day, I did it again and again. These were moments of normalcy. These were moments of hope. We could both relax and see daylight in the darkness again!

These special times helped us overcome. They helped us momentarily heal the heartless acts of staff who were in the wrong business.

Dehumanizing - Tactic or Stupidity?

Hall discovered that the sickest patients are the least liked by doctors and that very sick people sense this disaffection. (Groopman, 2007)

Isolation and aloneness quickly became the norm for Jay and I. Within the first few hours after diagnosis, negative information bombarded us. The moment our minds cleared, we acknowledged that aggressive cancer was a formidable opponent.

However, it took us a little longer to realize that cancer was secondary to an even more powerful, more menacing foe - the *American healthcare system.*

Our greatest adversary, the American healthcare system, gave us no time. It immediately screamed at us, pounded us, and got in our faces, pushing Jay to forfeit life and submit to a disease he had just encountered. We didn't understand it, we hadn't fully acknowledged it, and we hadn't had time to assimilate it.

The hostility, aggression, and isolation we felt the medical system hurled at us, however, didn't weaken us. It cemented our personal wills. It sealed the protective gear around us. Jay and I were connected. We strengthened the bond. We enhanced the love. We embraced the hope!

"I'm not ready to submit," Jay said. "I will acknowledge the crisis, but I want to focus on life. I want to live until I die!"

Once Jay established this 'go forth' strategy, a freight train coming full speed down the tracks would not stop me from carrying out his wishes. Our lives merged into a new dimension. Our time, our love, our relationship were more precious, more loving, and more fulfilling.

In fact, our relationship may have reached a pinnacle few others will ever understand. Giving in to the doctors and the hospitals would have meant giving up the very essence of who we were.

Our new resolve gave us the fortitude to fight, to ignore, to pity those who didn't know or understand. We were determined to stay the course.

Jay received the 'cold' treatment again and again. They came in pairs. They didn't smile or say, "Good morning, Jay." They didn't even acknowledge a person there with a simple nod of their heads.

But as they stood beside Jay's bed with his medicine in their hands, one looked at the other and said loudly and clearly, "He's a glio stage-four!" Then they turned and walked out the door.

Later, as the disease progressed, Jay's name changed. They didn't call him a "glio stage-four" anymore. He became a "glio *end-stage.*"

I began to know them. I could hear their words before they said them. Once they confirmed my fears with the dreaded glio announcement, I knew Jay was immaterial. He would receive ill-treatment instead of treatment, impatience instead of patience, and crudeness instead of care.

At first Jay and I tried to give these 'people' the benefit of the doubt. However, we finally concluded these untrained, undisciplined, uncaring, staff thought Jay was deaf, they thought his brain was mustard inside his head, or they were on a mission to dehumanize him.

If the reason for the ill-treatment was the latter of the three, an important question surfaced. Who was the director of the dehumanizing tactic, the hospital, the doctor, the insurance company?

Rhonda, who had worked in long-term care for eighteen years, reiterated often, "Mom, it's called Managed Care!"

Whether the atrocity was planned, whether it was the crux of the ignorant, referring to a patient as his disease rather than addressing him by name is unconscionable, inflicting great harm upon the patient, his family, and the profession for which the health care professional represents.

This travesty was by far the worst violation to Jay's psyche; it was the worst flagrant disconnect our family endured throughout our entire holocaustic experience.

Jay communicated fluently with family. He communicated in a more guarded manner with friends. However, he never communicated, by choice, with medical staff. He felt they didn't appreciate him and they didn't want to serve him. However, most importantly, he knew he didn't have the skills to interrupt them

23

and correct them!

So the sad, truthful irony is documented in the medical records. While medical staff treated Jay like a deaf, mute imbecile, family and friends were communicating with him both fluently and satisfactorily.

One day two friends came to see Jay. "Barbara is fighting for your life, Jay. Do you realize that?" they asked. Jay cried and let them know that he did understand. Later, when our church deacons came to our home to lay hands on him to pray for healing, Jay said, "My wife is fighting the fight and I don't know what I would do without her."

The first and most powerful oxymoron that Jay was forced to endure was the "first do no harm" lament. It was truly a lament, an ongoing chorus soliciting our family to view no care as comfort care.

Doctors chant the 'first do no harm' phrase in the name of the Hippocratic Oath. However, even though Hippocrates did make this statement at some point in his life, it was never a part of the Hippocratic Oath.

In addition, most doctors today don't even accept or adhere to the "Oath" as originally written. They either subscribe to a newer, later version of the Hippocratic Oath that incorporates modern day medical philosophy or they don't subscribe to any oath at all.

Therefore, many doctors who misquote the Hippocratic Oath are either fulfilling a hidden agenda or they are protecting their own apathetic intentions *to do nothing*.

Whatever the reasons, they are underestimating their own potential to heal or to make a difference, their patient and his family's intelligence, and the majesty and power of God.

Lazy In-Box Thinking

This is a fundamental schism in the field of oncology, between those who are driven almost entirely by data and those who are willing to treat patients outside of proven protocols. (Groopman, 2007)

The oncologist announced, "We will be giving Jay radiation and the chemotherapy drug, Temodar. This is 'state-of-the-art' treatment for the glioblastoma. It is the national protocol and the best we have. Temodar has only been around for the past few years. Before that, we had nothing."

"I proposed putting Jay in a study," the oncologist continued. "However, he didn't meet the criteria so he didn't qualify. The doctor declined to discuss the study any further."

I was astonished that Jay had seen an oncologist, neurologist, radiologist, doctor of internal medicine, and had an established cardiologist and no one was talking to anyone. No options were expressed, no possibilities were discussed. If the subject didn't include information regarding Jay's demise, the universal word was 'mum'!

"When I worked for the school district," I often begged the doctors, "we staffed complicated cases. The school psychologist, the principal, the teachers, the athletic trainers all met to confer, to brainstorm, to come up with innovative strategies for success. Please, can't we bring all the doctors' brilliance into one room and work toward the best outcome?"

"When I worked for the State of Kansas," I continued, "if we had a complicated food stamp case or Medicaid case, we would staff. The case worker, the supervisor, the area director, and maybe central office staff would confer, brainstorm, to come up with the best solution.

Is Jay's situation not as important as a school child's education or a person's food stamp case? Why," I begged, "won't the doctors communicate?"

"We are!" The oncologist snapped. "We all write notes on the patient log in the computer. We communicate on the computer."

"Jay and I aren't on the computer," I thought. "You aren't talking to us. It's Jay's life. Do you not know that communication is circular, not linear? Was Leo Buscaglia correct when he said, *"All our knowledge brings us nearer to our ignorance? Where is the wisdom we have lost in our knowledge?"*

I wondered: Did the medical doctors provide team-care for Bob Woodruff because he was an ABC News correspondent, because he was famous, or because the medics wanted personal fame and glory?

If we consider the statistics cited earlier, that 96% of the wounded soldiers reaching front-line medic centers survive, it appears top-notch care is extended to all.

However, according to news reports, investigations, and whistle blowers, increased infection, increased complications, and increased mortality occur *after* the soldiers return to the United States.

Even though Jay was not a talker, he was keenly aware. He knew the system was fighting against him, and he knew that he was vulnerable and defenseless. When medical staff entered the room, he clung to me. He didn't want me to leave his side. If I left the room for only a few minutes, he cried.

Jay knew that I loved him. He knew I was trying to protect him. He knew I would and could remove anyone from his room who violated him.

Visitors often remarked about the change in Jay's demeanor when hospital staff was near. "Jay stiffens up and has fear in his eyes when staff enters the room," they said.

Jay and I knew we were caught in a white-coat war zone. We began to check every smile, asking: "Is it genuine? Is it mercenary?" We began to question every order, watching for ulterior motives. The strain was 24/7. I began to have nightmares.

They were real. They were frightening. They were constant. One night-time terror just kept playing over and over in my head.

I saw clear, crisp visions of Jay's doctors fishing from their fancy yachts, trying to land the prize fish. I saw them persevering, sweating, trying to impress their equally wealthy and politically powerful 'friends.'

When these same men finished their play and put their trophies out for display, they returned to the hospital corridors. There a true metamorphosis took place. The doctors became small, insignificant beings. Their prowess dissipated. Their dexterity, ingenuity, and drive expired. Their little white coats that covered their muscles and their tans suddenly, abruptly turned from white to a bloody, fire red.

I searched for the cause. The audience was gone. The show had ended. Was it a test? What would they do left to their own conscience, left to their own breadth? Yes, at the first sign of medical crises, they turned and ran away from the bed!

Injuring the Injured

Each of us is unique in our biology, and there can be important differences in both the side-effects we suffer and the benefits we gain from the same medication. We can share a single illness but not share its remedy, despite receiving the same drug or undergoing the same procedure. (Groopman, 2007)

When Jay was ready to leave the ICU (Intensive Care Unit) following the brain biopsy, they moved him to a room directly across from the nurses' station. One nurse explained: "We need to watch Jay closely. He must not fall or bump his head," she said.

Jay continued to receive the Dylantin drip to prevent seizures, and it continued to deplete his senses, emotionality, and recovery. Staff continued to ignore the drug's impact. I did not!

I complained to whomever would listen. I explained that Jay and I didn't smoke. We didn't consume alcohol. Our bodies were not acclimated to medication.

"Maybe Jay can't tolerate the dose of Dylantin that others tolerate," I said. "Please double-check the Dylantin level in his blood. Please make sure that it is correct." I told every medical professional that came into the room. I begged, I pleaded, I cajoled.

Jay did well the first thing in the morning. He would get up and walk to the bathroom. He would eat a good breakfast. He talked. He always asked, "When will they let us go home?" However, immediately after they started the Dylantin drip, everything changed. He couldn't stand and he couldn't communicate. He became delirious.

One day a friend came to see us. She is a nurse and I wanted to visit with her privately. I didn't want to burden Jay with my questions and concerns. So we decided to visit in the little waiting room at the end of the hall.

I went to the nurses' station and said:

"I am going to the waiting room at the end of this hall to visit with my friend."

Then, holding up both my hands, spreading all ten fingers before their faces, I continued, "I will be gone ten minutes. *Ten minutes*," I said bouncing my ten fingers at them. "You must watch Jay. He is delirious from his Dylantin. He will try to get up. You must watch him."

"We'll watch him," the nurses all chimed.

In ten minutes, my friend and I returned to Jay's room. All overhead flood lights were on over his bed. Several nurses were standing over him, searching his head and body for injury!

No bed warning was set. No nurse watched. No care was given. Jay had fallen, pulled the IV out of his arm, and bruised his hip.

The truth had presented itself. They could no longer deny it. Belatedly, staff put two signs on the door outside Jay's room. They read "*Critical Incident*" and "*Low Stimulus: Brain Trauma Patient.*"

The next morning was a good morning. Jay walked to the bathroom. He ate a good breakfast. We laughed together. We cried together. He begged to go home again.

The rehabilitation technician came to the room and worked with Jay a few moments. Then she said, "I was going to walk Jay down the hall this morning, but he can't walk."

"Yes, he can," I snapped. "He did it this morning with ease."

"Well," she said, "he is just pushing up against me."

I looked into Jay's eyes. They were glassy and fixed. I saw that he was pushing hard against the technician. I looked at the medicine dispenser beside his bed. "Oh, my, gosh," I wailed. "They started the Dylantin drip. He's sick; please lay him down."

A little later a neurosurgeon came to Jay's room on morning rounds. I walked over to him and said, "Sir, I have a question for you this morning."

"What is the question," he said with audible disgust.

"I'm wondering why we are giving Jay his Dylantin drip

before he is scheduled to work with rehabilitation. He functions fine first thing in the morning. However, after he receives the drip, he can no longer function at all. Is it possible to change the schedule . . . ."

Before I could finish my sentence, the doctor screeched, "I am not going to argue with you!" Then he abruptly turned, pointed at the nurse, and barked, "Take down the Dylantin drip!"

I snapped to defensive attention and pointed to the nurse in response. "Don't take down the Dylantin drip," I ordered.

Then looking back at the doctor, I said, "Doctor, I was simply asking you if we could reevaluate the procedure. I didn't ask you to jeopardize my husband's care."

Jay began to sob. The neurosurgeon, the person, the department that ordered the *"low stimulus, brain trauma patient"* sign on the door, was yelling at me in front of my gravely ill husband and his guests. The doctor, in his tirade, was oblivious to Jay's trauma and emotional pain.

Wrapped up in his tirade, integrated into his own monologue, the doctor raised his right foot knee-high off the floor, arched his right arm halo fashion over his head, and stiffened and separated his fingers into a claw-like position. He stood in this lunging position beside Jay's hospital bed, yelling at me,"I am not going to argue with you! Nurse, take down the Dylantin drip."

Half-dozen guests sat agape, listening to the outburst. The nurse was visibly shaken. I was becoming extremely angry.

"Doctor," the nurse said with tears in her eyes, "do you want me to take it down now? It is half administered. His wife is right, doctor. The minute we begin the drip, you can see the patient descend into delirium."

"Don't remove the Dylantin drip," I ordered again!

Shela walked across the room and stood beside me for support. I looked at the doctor and demanded. "We need to go into the hall to discuss this further." We left the room.

The neurologist said, "If you aren't happy with what we're doing, you can go somewhere else."

"I had a patient once," he continued. "The patient had a deep-seated brain tumor. I wouldn't operate on it. He went to another doctor and they did operate on it. As far as I know, he's still alive."

"Well, doctor," I said with sarcasm. "If you referred that man for the life-saving treatment, congratulations; if you didn't refer him for the treatment, shame on you!"

"As far as changing doctors, finding a neurosurgeon isn't like going from K-mart to Walmart to Target, sir. My husband is desperately ill! He needs the best of the best. I will take him anywhere he needs to go; I just need to know where that place is!"

The next morning, an oncologist came into Jay's room and sat beside his bed. He sat there looking into Jay's eyes without comment. Then he turned to me and said, "The neurosurgeon called me last night. He told me that you attacked him yesterday."

I laughed in disgust. "Really," I asked? "Actually, I asked him a question. However, there were several guests in the room. After the doctor's tirade, one guest remarked," 'Gee, I didn't know a four-year-old could become a neurosurgeon. That 'child' has some r-e-a-l issues!' "

"Well," the oncologist answered. "You do need to know that if you push too hard, we'll push back!"

"Why does this remark not surprise me," I thought. Then I asked, "What does that mean?"

He didn't answer, but went on to say, "I referred you to the neurosurgeon that I did because of temperament. If you think the doctor you visited with yesterday is bad, there are others you certainly wouldn't want to meet.

Later that morning, I asked the nurse why Jay was not receiving the Dylantin drip. "The rehabilitation doctor ordered a blood test," she answered. "The test revealed that Jay has too high concentration of Dylantin in his blood. The doctor ordered to dispense with the next two doses and then begin the drip again at half the dose."

"Praise, God!" I said. "Someone cared enough to ask some questions and get some answers. Amazing! It was rehabilitation who initiated change; it wasn't the neurosurgeon."

Neglect Rubs Salt on the Illness Wound
Humiliation is the loss of dignity. (Stein, 2007)

The night nurse came into the room and helped Jay to the bathroom. She stood there a short time. Then she said, "I'm going to step out for a moment. I'll be back soon."

I remained at Jay's side several more minutes. We talked. Several minutes grew into more minutes. When the nurse didn't return, I looked out the door.

I saw her sitting there with others at the nurses' station. Her back was toward Jay's door. The chatting was low key, sprinkled with a sporadic giggle or two.

At first, I thought about asking her if she remembered Jay. I thought about asking her to come help us. But then my mind said, "No. I am tired. I am tired of the battle. I am tired of trying to make irresponsible people responsible. Let her have her freedom. Let her go."

Instead, I returned to the bathroom and said, "Hey, Sweetheart, you ready to go back to bed?"

"Yes," he said with a big sigh of relief.

Together, holding tight to one another, we walked back to bed. He snuggled in between the sheets, turned over, and closed his eyes. I climbed into my bed, the recliner chair. We drifted into a fitful sleep.

Suddenly, around 11:00 p.m. the door burst open. The nurse ran frantically to the bathroom. She gasped. Then she looked around the dark room. "Oh, my, gosh," she said. "You put him back to bed!"

"Yes," I mumbled, "about three hours ago!"

Men of the 'Shroud'

A doctor's strength determines a patient's protection. Doctors need to understand that the loneliness of illness is a state of loss and surrender, and they must know how to protect the sick and fight for them, even if they can't rescue them. Doctors must lend strength in the form of optimism. Optimism can mock death and weakness. (Stein, 2007)

Jay began radiation and chemotherapy. The relief that we were now doing something to fight the cancer allowed me to focus on complementary health strategies. I began to research. The American Cancer Society information recommended exercise to help alleviate weakness and fatigue in patients receiving chemotherapy. So after Jay's daily radiation treatments, we went to the Heart Center to exercise.

Health care professionals are always at the Heart Center, watching and assisting patients. So we walked the track. We rode the recumbent bikes, and we did arm exercises. Jay worked out ten to thirty minutes, depending upon his fatigue level. I stayed very close to him. He looked over at me periodically, smiling with reassurance. This was a great time for us. It was a partnership. It was a blessing.

The oncologist, who prescribed Jay's chemotherapy drug, Temodar, was unavailable. Even though he had prescribed two powerful drugs for Jay, Temodar and Decadron (Dexamethasone) to reduce brain swelling, he didn't schedule an appointment, he didn't schedule any blood tests, he didn't visit with us about medicinal side-effects. It was if he 'vanished without a trace.'

Perhaps his workload was massive, perhaps it was oversight due to more pressing things on the agenda, or maybe it was fulfilling prophesy 'to push back.' For whatever reason, we never saw him again.

We were seeing a competent, caring radiologist at this time. He obviously was thinking of the oncologist also because he asked: "How are you and Jay's oncologist getting along?"

"Fine," I said, "You can't fight with someone you never see."

"He hasn't called you?" he asked.

"Not once," I said, "Jay's about half-way through his treatment now, isn't he?"

"Yes," he answered, "I'll call the oncologist today and tell him to call you."

It was amazing to me that another doctor must suggest the oncologist visit with his own patient -- a patient who was taking two extremely powerful drugs that he prescribed!

A short time later, Jay began to lose weight. It seemed the weight slid from his body. He became lethargic and he just wanted to stay in bed. I expressed my concerns to the radiologist and he ordered a blood test.

The results revealed Jay's blood sugar was elevated. The radiologist said Jay had chemically induced diabetes caused by the Decadron. So he referred him to an endocrinologist.

A new battle ensued.

The endocrinologist prescribed Novolog 70/30. She said the Diabetic Learning Center would call us for an appointment. However, in the meantime I consulted my pharmacist. "I am having trouble keeping Jay's blood sugar stable," I said. "What does Novolog 70/30 mean anyway?"

"It means that 70% of the drug works within the first hour," he explained. "Thirty percent becomes effective five to six hours later. You also might keep in mind that a person's blood sugar may dip to a lower level during the night hours."

That explained it. Jay's blood sugar did dip into the lower numbers during the nighttime. Every morning it was below the normal blood sugar range of 90 to 110. It was consistently in the 50's and 60's. I called the endocrinologist.

"Jay's blood sugar is very low in the mornings," I said. "I travel alone with Jay and I don't want his blood sugar to dip too low. Can he tolerate a little higher blood sugar? Can we shoot for 130 or less? Please, he doesn't need the trauma from insulin shock."

The endocrinologist made no adjustments. One morning Jay's blood sugar registered 50. I called the office again. I said, "Jay's blood sugar is 50 this morning. I just want you to know that I am *not* going to give Jay 15 units of insulin when he has a 50 blood sugar!"

The nurse sarcastically replied, "Well, you're supposed to!"

"Well, I'm not going to!" I countered.

Later another nurse called me and we worked through the momentary crises. However, Jay's blood sugar continued to dip dangerously low from time to time.

Finally, Jay's radiation therapy was almost completed. He had one more treatment scheduled for the following day. A new radiologist was assigned to us so we met with him for Jay's dismissal. "What comes next?" I asked.

"Nothing," he emphasized! Then accusingly he added, "If it were my wife, I would go home and call family and friends. But I can see you are not going to do that. . ."

"No, sir, we are not," I assured him, "because you're *not* God."

I knew my remark would bring reprimands. I knew it would bring verbal thrashings. However, I really didn't care. The onslaught designed to weaken our resolve was heavy and continual. I no longer had patience. I had learned to speak as swiftly and plainly as the offense. It was a matter of survival.

So I wasn't surprised the next morning when a 'Man of the Cloth,' a minister, entered the waiting room. His presence was par. Breech staff was diligent about calling the clergy every time I upset the doctors, disagreed with them, or challenged them.

Jay and I made a joke of it. "The clergy are tools," we said. "They are institutional puppets, helping Breech make a point. They are essential to the hospital cause. They ensure the death protocol will not fail."

Even though Jay was aware of the situation, even though he could see through the facade, I was relieved the radiology therapists had called him back for his last treatment. I wouldn't have to watch my tongue to protect Jay. I could say exactly what was on my mind.

The clergy looked to one side of the waiting room and said, "Good morning." Then he looked to the other side of the waiting room and said, "Hello." However, his steps were straight; his gait never faltered. He was pointed directly at me. When he sat beside me wearing a *"well, imagine you being here"* attitude, I didn't waste time.

"Before you begin," I pleaded, "listen to what I have to say.

Please understand that I am not comparing Jay or myself with Christ. He is the King of Kings. He is I Am. He is the Creator, the Savior, the Prince of Peace.

Jay and I are only tiny pebbles of sand among all the other tiny pebbles of sand on earth. However, scripture indicates that Christ wasn't looking forward to his crucifixion. When he was in the garden, he sweat blood. He called out to the Father saying, "If it is your will, please take this cup from me."

"Yes," the clergyman said, "but He knew when to say '"*It is Finished*!'"

"You're right, sir," I slammed back. "But Christ knew it was finished because of His relationship with the Father. He knew it was finished because the plan was perfect. He knew it was finished because He was fully God and fully Man. But, sir, he certainly didn't ask Breech oncologists and radiologists if it was finished, and *Jay and I aren't going to either!*"

Jay and I left Breech Medical Center that day depressed and defeated.

Lies, Lies, and More Lies Exposed

During an illness there is really only one choice - to proceed or not to proceed. And not proceeding is giving up. (Stein, 2007)

Jay and I went home. I began to make telephone calls. I called the National Brain Tumor Foundation. I called numerous cancer centers. I called a local medical doctor who practiced alternative medicine.

The National Brain Tumor Foundation provided names and telephone numbers of people who had survived the glioblastoma. These people gave the Foundation permission for people to call them and talk to them. I called them. I listened. I learned. The survivors' stories made a mockery of the doctors' hype - "no one has ever survived the glioblastoma!"

None of the survivors I visited with knew about the drug Temodar. Each of them had taken other drugs. One survivor told me that she became so ill at one point that she was having seizures on top of seizures. She said, "In the beginning, I also had a defeatist doctor. He told my family, "'if you think your loved one is going to come out of this - think again. She is not. She is dying!'"

"By God's mercy we had an Angel," she added. "One doctor was not willing to give up. He watched me, he worked with me, he stayed by me and here I am today."

The consistent message among the brain tumor survivors was the caliber of their doctors. The survivors described their attending physicians as optimistic, daring, and unafraid to step on the edge of treatment. They used unconventional methods, tried drug cocktails, and unabashedly maintained life through supports at deadly, crucial times. "They were Angels of Mercy," the survivors asserted.

The contrast between the survivors' doctors and Jay's doctors appalled me. Jay's doctors were defeated from day one. There was only one plan; the plan that Jay should die as quickly as possible. They didn't watch him closely or provide supportive medications to help him tolerate chemotherapy. They didn't have plan B when Temodar lost its punch. They never entertained the thought of cocktail drugs. Every time I asked, "What can we do next?" Their emphatic reply was "Nothing!" I had to beg and fight for every morsel, for every tidbit that Jay received.

I shared the glioblastoma survivor stories with Jay's doctors. "After hearing the survivors' stories, the difference in healing appears to be the difference in approach." I said. "Please, if you have ever wanted to try something different, if you have ever thought you could make strides against this beast, please, do it now! We are giving you our permission. We are sanctioning a go ahead."

They ridiculed me. They discounted me. They argued their point without reservation. "Studies show," they gloated, "that people who survived a brain tumor didn't have a glioblastoma after all. They may have originally diagnosed it as a glioblastoma, but in every case, they later found that it was something else; it - - really - - wasn't - - a - - glioblastoma."

"Whatever," I said. "But you must admit the standard approach to the glioblastoma is not aggressive. It is defensive rather than offensive. If Jay had leukemia, you would hospitalize him and treat him close to death. You would monitor him, support him, and be at his side throughout the ordeal. With the glioblastoma, you give some medication and send him home to die."

"You aren't even being realistic here," they blasted. "You are comparing apples to oranges. The glioblastoma is not leukemia. It is a glioblastoma! We know more about how to cure leukemia; we are trekking new ground with the glioblastoma."

"No, sir, I am not comparing two different things here," I cried in exasperation. "I am comparing attitude and approach to attitude and approach. The disease I mentioned is immaterial. It's the medical *state-of-mind* and *defensive approach* we are discussing."

The door was closed. The doctors refused our pleas. They wouldn't venture away from the national protocol. They were stuck in their own simple-mindedness.

The doctor apparently had not read his own specialty medical journal because according to the *Journal of Clinical Oncology*, a few patients have survived the Glioblastoma Mediforme. So Jay and I were forced to move on in other ways.

We made an appointment with a medical doctor with expertise in alternative medicine. He counseled that since the doctors refused to prescribe vitamins, minerals, and other nutritional supports for Jay, we should juice fresh fruits and vegetables every day. "This enhanced nutrition won't interfere with his other medical regimen." He said.

We bought a juicer and Jay thrived. Our faithful church family brought us fresh vegetables and fruits each week. They brought oranges, apples, carrots, spinach, every berry, and more. Jay's cheeks became rosy and he gained strength.

We found a massage therapist who was a retired nurse. She had expertise in giving massages to cancer patients. Jay loved going for a massage. He closed his eyes and relaxed while I sat in the corner of the room sobbing. The soft music, watching my best friend rest in peace, and whispering my fears to God were too much for me. I sat trembling as the tears flowed.

One evening Jay said, "You know what?"

"No, Jay," I answered, "what?"

"I think I would like to take water therapy."

"You would," I asked in surprise. "I actually thought of that, but you have always been afraid of water. I decided it might be more traumatic than helpful."

"I don't think so," he said. "If somebody is in the water with me, I don't think that I would be afraid."

"Okay, let's go for it," I said.

The Great Becomes Ordinary

Belief and expectation - the key elements of hope - can block pain by releasing endorphins and enkephalins mimicking the effects of morphine. In some cases, hope can also have important effects on fundamental physiological processes like respiration, circulation, and motor function. During an illness, then, hope can be imagined as a domino effect, a chain reaction in which each link makes improvement more likely. It changes us profoundly in spirit and body. (Groopman, 2004)

Jay's and my next maneuver, our next search for hope, for understanding, for treatment was J.R. Cancer Center in Texas. I had visions of meeting an extraordinary doctor - a doctor who could give us peace and hope.

As we prepared for the trip, Jay looked at me with tears in his eyes. "You know," he said, "that I can't help you find the way."

"Oh, dear, God," I prayed in silence. "My dear, sweet best friend can't help find the way. My husband who worked for KDOT, my sweetheart who never needed help to reach a destination, my rock who understood the spider web of highways and byways, connections and crossways, the man whose hobby was to follow roads to see where they lead, said he can't find the way!"

My heart went out to him. I held him. I reassured him. I joked with him and laughed with him. All the while, I was praying in my heart, "Dear Lord, have mercy on my precious husband. Please touch his soul. Give him grace and peace and comfort. Please be with us, Lord, as we take this trip, I pray."

"It's okay, Jay," I said. "I can make it. I can make it because you will be at my side. We're a team. Watch out Texas, here we come."

Everything on the trip went smoothly. When we successfully traveled through Dallas, Texas, Jay gave a sigh of relief and said, "You made it!"

That evening when we stopped at the motel, Jay was acting strangely. It was as if he was drifting instead of walking. "Jay," I asked, "is everything okay?"

"No," he said, "something is wrong. I can't walk. I can't see."

I quickly took him back to our room and tested his blood sugar. "Oh, no, your blood sugar is under 40!" I cried. "Jay, here is some pudding. Please eat it quickly." Then I began to shovel spoons of the sweet antidote into his mouth.

After Jay stabilized, I said, "I am not going to give you any more insulin. We will be at the hospital tomorrow. You're just in for protein treats until we get there, ol' buddy. No more carbohydrates for you."

At J.R. Cancer Center, Jay walked the long maze of hallways to the oncology department. When we were called to the examining room, he sat in a chair in the middle of the room most accessible to the doctor. I sat in a chair in the corner.

The physician assistant walked into the room. She didn't speak to Jay, but looked directly at me. "When the tumor is in this location in the brain, patients have the tendency to pull away from family and friends. Has Jay done that yet?"

Jay immediately began to sob. I went to him and held his trembling body. My mouth was agape, my mind was in shock, my spirit was crushed. If I were not a lady, I would have punched her in the mouth. We drove over 1000 miles and were spending over $1,000 for this? The first thing *"the place to go"* institution had to offer was to take away Jay's last thread of hope. The last thing on this earth that Jay would ever want was to pull away from family and friends!

My answer was curt, definite, and accusing. "No," I said. "And he will not do that - end of subject!"

The doctor walked in. He sat on a chair facing Jay. "I must tell you the truth," he said.

"Please, don't," my mind was saying. "You must know Jay has heard this *truth* over and over again. Every single doctor felt he must tell him 'the truth'. Please dear God, please dear God, don't let them do this to Jay again." But the conversation continued.

"I must tell you that you are terminal," he continued.

Jay began to sob again. "That means that I have two months to live," Jay cried.

"Who told you that?" the doctor questioned.

"My doctors at home told me," Jay answered.

"Well, any doctor who would give you a time limit is fooling himself," he said. "Doctors can't determine the year, the day, the hour that patients will or will not die."

But then as if the angel of death put a stab in the doctor's rib, he added, "However, older patients do tend to die sooner than younger patients with this tumor."

I winced! That last stab seemed to be important to the doctor. It seemed to be necessary. It seemed to guarantee the doctor's compliance with the 'death culture.' However, a fifth grader could see that the last statement was unnecessary. It was said for the doctor's benefit, not the patient's.

The only purpose it could have for the patient was negative. It could destroy any ray of hope, it could help rip away the right to focus on life, it could mock his motto to live until he died.

What does the patient care about statistics? What does he care about numbers? This is *his* life. This is *his* fight. All he wants to do is to concentrate on his life, his support, and his personal possibilities.

"It won't benefit you to stay here," the doctor said. "I am willing to work with a doctor in Kansas." Then he turned to me and added, "I want you to wean Jay off the Decadron. This drug is for brain swelling and Jay doesn't have any brain swelling. It will only decrease his strength, thin out his skin, and make him wheelchair bound sooner."

"Also, don't give him anymore insulin at this time. Just monitor his food intake until you return home."

When we left the hospital, we were more confused than when we arrived. I couldn't foresee the arrogant oncologist we knew at home working with another doctor of our choice. We were intent, we were concerned, and we were broken all the way home.

Angels Among Us

The team of doctors had found scientific articles that reported on how the deficiency of even a single vitamin could impair immune function. (Groopman, 2007)

The richness of friendship, the intimacy of touch, the tenderness from strangers bolstered Jay and I, allowing us to bask in rare moments of warmness. These angels with invisible wings provided the necessary nutrients for our souls to get up again, to care again, to forge forward again.

As we traveled to J.R. Cancer Center from our home, people we didn't know, people we will never know, people we wouldn't recognize again, touched us and smiled at us. They didn't care if Jay had a glioblastoma. They didn't notice anything wrong with his head. They simply saw a couple that could use a helping hand.

They smiled and greeted us. They put their groceries aside; many put them on the ground to help Jay get into the Cougar. They held doors open for us so Jay and I could enter the store in an embrace rather than one after the other. They gave us directions and sometimes even led the way. I know that we will all meet once again, Jay, me, and them. And I can thank them once again!

Long-time friends are a blessing. They know when the rope is short. They are there at off-times and on-times and in-between times. They call. They show-up. They send cards. They know what you are feeling without asking. Jay and I had a friend like that.

Joyce and I were grade school friends, high school friends, and are now adult-time friends. The camaraderie between us is complete. Time during Jay's illness was incidental. If we needed a friend to talk to, 4:00, 6:00, 3:00, a.m. or p.m., whatever, whichever, whenever, we knew she was there.

When pomegranate season ended in Kansas, Joyce's state still boasted a few. So she gathered a boxful of these antioxidant wonders and mailed them to us, helping Jay enjoy fresh pomegranate juice for a few weeks longer.

This fruit and all the fresh fruit and vegetables our church family brought every week, was *real* comfort care for Jay. They helped heal, support, and reenergize his body. We could see it, we could measure it, and Jay could feel it.

There were others too. They mowed and trimmed our yard, trees, and shrubs, keeping the yard healthy and clean.

And then there was the couple who often came by,   cleaning the garage, sitting with Jay, changing outdoor lights, and styling my hair. They were indispensable.

Something was unique about all these people. They weren't trying. They weren't measuring. They weren't competing. They were just being.

Money, Politics, and Power

Whenever consolation arrives, it comes not from an answer but from being heard. (Stein, 2007)

When we returned home, we made an appointment with our internist. We asked him for a referral to another oncologist. At first, he argued. "Your oncologist will work with J.R. Cancer Center." However, after further conversation, he reluctantly acquiesced.

"We want someone who will support us," I explained to the new oncologist.

"I'll support you," he said with no inflection, with no emotion.

Then he warned," I'm going to continue to give Jay Decadron. Period. I don't care who said to take him off it."

"The Cancer Center told us that the drug will hinder Jay's ability to be mobile. They also said that 12 to 16 milligrams is a powerful dose, suggesting 4 milligrams may be more tolerable.

Please explain why you think Jay should continue to take Decadron at this high dose." I said.

"Because people tend to do better when they are on it," he snapped.

"Better? How?" I questioned.

"They just do better," he repeated. He refused to provide any more information.

"Well, I guess my next question is: Will you work with the doctor at the Cancer Center?"

"He isn't very interested in working with anyone here. We haven't heard a thing from him." he said.

"We haven't had a home doctor who was even interested in Jay's case and no one has been willing to refer us to someone who cares. I didn't know a doctor's name to give the Cancer Center. Are you willing to work with them or not?" I quizzed.

"I will tell you one thing," he said without answering my question. "I won't take Jay off Decadron. You can take it or leave it!"

When Jay and I left the office, we were both crying. We wanted to get to the car before too many people noticed us. We knew at that very moment we weren't going back. He said we could take it or leave it. We were going to leave it!

This appointment was like all Jay's other appointments with local doctors. He didn't ask Jay any questions. He didn't touch him or relate to him. He sat and looked at him.

As always, the encounter seemed eerie to us, talking *about* Jay, *about* his condition, *about* his feelings. It was as if Jay were invisible, eavesdropping on his own conversation. We talked about this every time we returned home from one of these empty seat sessions.

"They're stiff shirts," Jay would say. "They just ignore me. They think I am dead already. I can't think fast enough to tell them what I want." Then he would cry.

I sat with him and I held him, all the while talking to the doctors in my head:

"And you say that you 'first do no harm'? Your uncouth manner, your negligence, your arrogance your simple-mindedness will be the very death of my husband. You *are* doing him harm! You are slowly killing him with your vile nature!"

The Deserter - the Coward's Coward

The mantra "It's a bad disease" can shift the burden off the specialist. Instead of struggling to come at the malady from a different angle, seeking its vulnerable point by adding other drugs or customizing a regimen, the physician, in essence surrenders. (Groopman, 2007)

Our doctor of alternative medicine suggested an oncologist in a neighboring town. I made an appointment with the oncologist and signed Jay up for an introductory session in rehabilitation.

We had just finished eating breakfast and Jay was sitting in his recliner. His teeth clenched. His eyes blinked incessantly and one side of his face began to contract and relax. He was having a seizure! I called 911.

The emergency room doctor gave us another reprieve from the medical battering. We discussed Jay's condition and his daily routine. We talked about his water therapy. I explained Jay's problem with Dylantin.

"When Jay was in the hospital for his brain biopsy, the doctors told me there was no other drug to prevent seizures. What are we going to do?" I asked.

"That is incorrect information," the doctor answered. "I don't know why they told you that. There are many drugs that effectively control seizures." He prescribed one of those drugs and we went home.

Jay experienced one more seizure a few days later. Then the day that Jay was to meet his new rehabilitation therapist, he began to walk in a scissor gait, unable to keep his balance. We decided to keep the appointment anyway.

We looked at each other and promised, "We can do this. We can walk to the car and drive to the rehab-hospital." So we put our arms around each other and held very, very tightly. We took tiny steps. We stopped. Then we started again. With love and will, we made it.

Then to get into the front seat of our Mercury Cougar, Jay needed to keep his torso high enough to sit in the seat, but his head low enough to miss the upper door frame. It took a raise-lower movement. Together, we up-downed correctly, maneuvering him into the front seat. Then we took a minute to hold each other in relief.

Jay looked at me with depth, understanding, and passion. "I am sad," he said. "You are becoming my slave."

"Jay," I countered. "When we love the Lord, we serve him because we love him. We become servants of the Lord. In that context, can you tell me the difference between a slave and a servant?"

"Yes," he said. "A slave is in bondage. A servant serves out of free will."

"You're right," I said, kissing him on the cheek. "So from now on when you think I am becoming your slave, just remember how much I love you and that I am serving you out of free will. I am here because *I want to be here!*"

My mind raced over the doctors' opinions of Jay. This conversation didn't mirror their beliefs, their predictions. Jay was not removed from reality. He was not withdrawing from loved ones. He was not incapable of thinking, wondering, caring, and feeling.

When we arrived at the new rehab-center, I had hospital volunteers bring a wheelchair to the car. This was the first time Jay used a wheelchair. I wheeled him into therapy.

"How did you get him here?" the rehabilitation therapist asked.

"We're a team," I answered. "We do what we need to do when we need to do it. We're here."

"Well, I can't allow you to leave with him when he is in this condition," she said. "I'm going to call the doctor."

The oncologist admitted Jay to the hospital. He told us that the tumor was advancing. He said, "In my opinion, Jay will be dead by the end of the week."

The oncologist talked to me about signing a "Do Not Resuscitate" (D & R) order. He didn't overtly pressure me. However, all the negative talk, all the badgering I had received for the past five months about my duty to save Jay from the disease was wearing on me - haunting me. The doctor promised to do everything, except resuscitate. This was the first doctor I trusted. I signed.

The nurses promptly put a D&R bracelet on Jay's arm. "Oh, Dear God," I instantly thought, "I just put the *mark* on my own husband. I designated him a leper - a person that no one can touch in crises."

I became sick. I thought I was going to vomit. I couldn't believe I had violated Jay's wishes to appease the system. How could I have done this? I was a traitor. I hated myself. I hated the system.

The oncologist took Jay off Novolog 70/30 and prescribed regular insulin. Nurses administered the insulin on a sliding scale. They didn't give Jay insulin if his blood sugar was under 150. This was a wonderful change. It eliminated the guess work and Jay's blood sugar began to stabilize.

Even though I was emphatic about Jay's continual pain-free status and even though Jay told staff that he was not hurting, the oncologist ordered pain relievers and the anti-anxiety medication, Ativan, for him anyway.

I was amazed that morphine was one the drugs the doctor prescribed. It was set up so the patient would receive a pre-set dose by pushing a button at bedside. However, Jay couldn't trip the apparatus, so the medication only was released by either the nurses or me.

Very quickly, Jay became extremely agitated. He began to experience sleep apnea. He couldn't lay still. He thrashed about, turning around and around in bed. He threw his blankets off. He grabbed at his hospital gown and succeeded in ripping it off many times. He tried to get up. He thrashed day and night.

One evening, a young, empathetic hospital aide said, "This is a man thing. Jay doesn't want that gown on. Let's take it off." He took Jay's gown and threw it in the laundry.

The hospital put an alarm on Jay's bed. They stationed sitters just outside his room to watch him so he wouldn't fall. Even though I felt down deep in my heart that Jay was receiving too many narcotics, it still seemed like heaven after being at Breech Medical Center. So I remained silent.

Staff was actually watching the patient. The oncologist had great bed-side manner, treating both Jay and I with respect. He shared many of his medical decisions with me and asked my permission to go forward. My defenses began to lower and I began to relax. However, this reprieve was short-circuited many times. It was a mirage that would soon entirely dissipate.

Jay quit thrashing and began to sleep. At that moment, I was relieved. "Maybe he's getting better," I thought.

However, I suddenly realized that I couldn't wake him. I remembered the doctor's prediction, "*I think Jay will be dead by the end of the week.*" I was terrified, wondering if Jay was descending into a comatose state.

Then the nurse came to me in tears. "I must tell you," she said. "I made a mistake when I gave Jay his medicine. I overdosed him. I told the doctor, and he said to put him on oxygen and watch him closely. He said that we need to keep Jay safe, but that he could use the sleep the medication will provide."

My heart sank. "Well," I responded, "I appreciate you coming directly to me. I'm not happy about it. But you could have hidden the fact from both the doctor and me. That would have put Jay in greater jeopardy than he is now. Please just watch him closely so we can get through this."

Jay's apnea was a direct result of his medication. It was easy to see this as time went on. I began to complain to the nurses. I urged them to quit using morphine and Ativan. As we reduced the dosages, Jay seemed to be getting better. He began to eat more of his meals.

However, Medicare was not going to pay for more care. Jay had to move off the ward. He was desperately ill! He had a deadly disease! But the 'rules' were against us. The money-changers wouldn't consider it. Jay was forced to leave.

A nurse came into the room to help Jay get up. Rhonda handed her the gate-belt, a wide belt designed to prevent falling and injury. "We don't need that," the nurse barked.

"To prevent injury, the family prefers you use the belt," Rhonda reiterated. "The gate-belt is mandated in some hospitals. Jay is extremely unstable right now. So please use it!"

"We know what we are doing here," the nurse barked back. She continued to move Jay without the belt. Rhonda assisted her for Jay's safety and for his sake.

The doctor discussed two possibilities for Jay's move - rehabilitation or swing bed. Since Jay couldn't pass the test to qualify for rehabilitation due to his apparent drugged state, we moved him to swing-bed.

The doctor arranged for us to move to a nice room with a couch, television, and motel atmosphere. He wanted Jay and I away from the other patients. He said, "You have enough to face with Jay's illness. I don't want you to have to deal with others' problems."

Jay slowly, steadily improved. I began to look forward rather than downward. I hated the D&R bracelet more and more. I thought about cutting it off his arm. If we got through this, if we made it out of here, I would never, never allow the D&R bracelet to be put on my precious sweetheart again. Never! I was beginning to look forward to a time to go home.

"Doctor," I said, "It is about time for Jay's next dose of Temodar. You are going to give it to him, aren't you? We can see instant improvement every time he takes the drug."

"If he can still swallow," he answered.

"Why won't you give it if he can't swallow?" I asked.

"Because pill form is the only way the drug is available," he answered. "Also, you will not see instant improvement with this cancer. If the cancer was lymphoma or some another type cancer, you might. However, it doesn't work that way with the glioblastoma."

"Whatever," I thought. "You weren't there and I'm not going to argue with you about it." For me, the push was on, however. The doctor told me what I had to do for Jay to receive the chemotherapy. I would see that it was done.

In that moment, in that instant, I knew Jay would swallow his Temodar. I worked with him every meal. Every day he improved. He finished all his meal, then he finished most of his meal, then he ate every spoonful again. He drank fluids well.

A turnaround began to take place. My greatest worry now was that Jay didn't use his right arm or leg. He acted as if they weren't there. However, this just increased my zeal. I knew Temodar was the answer of the moment. I knew I would see immediate results if I could give him the medication.

Suddenly, as I was helping Jay eat, he became drowsy. I worked and worked with him, but he kept falling asleep. Finally, he couldn't take another bite. The nurse came into the room. I complained, "Jay keeps falling asleep. I can't get him to eat."

"Oh," she said matter-of-factly, "I just tripped the morphine."

"You what!" I bellowed. "Why did you do that? He's not in pain. You knew it was dinner time. Why did you do that?"

Without acknowledging me, she left the room. I moved the dinner tray and helped Jay put his head back on his pillow. I sat down on the couch and sobbed.

The same nurse arrived the next day for duty. "Help," I cried to the family. "Every time this nurse is on duty, Jay is out." I told the other nurses. "Jay doesn't respond to noises, my touch, or my voice. He doesn't wake up at all when that nurse is on duty. She trips the morphine every chance she gets. I don't know what else she is changing in his medications."

The nurses were empathetic. "We know." They said. "We all

have problems with that nurse also. You have the right, you know, to remove her from your husband's care."

Suddenly, Jay began to moan. His eyes rolled back into his head. When he did look at me, he had fear in his eyes. I sat beside his bed. I held his hand and talked to him. Kevin and I both thought he was dying.

Kevin and I continued to work together, talking to Jay and encouraging him. We held his hands and rubbed his shoulders. We told him that we loved him. Then the morphine-tripping nurse came into the room. She frightened me because she had an eerie pity-smirk on her face.

Kevin and I stayed at Jay's side. We persevered for the next four hours. Finally, Jay began to settle. He became coherent again. I immediately vowed, "Whatever that nurse did today, she is not going to do it again." I officially kicked her out of Jay's room.

With the angel of death expelled, Jay continued to get better. Then it was time for Temodar. I wouldn't let anyone administer it, but myself. I didn't trust anyone else with my husband's pill for life.

The nurse brought the Temodar. I gave Jay his first dose. The next morning when I woke up, I sat on the couch and watched Jay. He pulled his right knee up. Then he crossed his left leg over it. He reached toward his foot and pulled his sock off with his right hand. "Praise God," I whispered. "Praise God for your wonderful healing power." Then I fell asleep again.

When the doctor came into the room later that morning, I exclaimed, "Guess what?"

"I know," he answered. "I came in earlier when both you and Jay were asleep. I saw Jay kicking off with his right foot."

We began to make plans to go home. The doctor and I visited about our plans. "Do you want hospice or a long-term care facility?" he asked.

"I certainly don't want hospice," I said, "and the only way Jay will ever go to long-term care is if I have a bed right beside his. I heard too many horror stories about long-term care when I worked for the state.

I also personally know about more than one case of physical abused in long-term care. The abuses were documented,

51

substantiated, and resulted in staff dismissal. The answer is no. I am going to take him home. He told me that he wants to go home."

"You won't be able to care for Jay by yourself," he argued. "I won't be on the team anymore. I am removing myself from Jay's case. So I won't be your doctor when you return home. He needs IV fluids and these fluids are very expensive."

"You just watch me," I said. "If you're pulling out, you owe us a referral. You said earlier that you knew doctors who would treat until the very last moment. That is who we want. Who are they?"

"No," he said, "I don't owe you a referral. You have good doctors in your home city. I will send your records anywhere you tell me to send them, but I will not give a referral."

I was so disturbed that I checked the Patients' Bill of Rights. The doctor was correct. He didn't have to provide a referral. The Patients' Bill of Rights only indicates that doctors must ensure continuity of care.

Little did I know at that time, the doctor was actually 'dumping' Jay on home health as Medicare demands. Home health, an under-funded, under-staffed and over-regulated agency, can only provide skeletal care at best. Jay and I quickly termed home health '*Mickey Mouse Medicine,*' mocking the continuity of care concept. However, with no other real choice, we chose home health services.

Our love-affair was over. The kind-hearted doctor, the 'king of bed-side manner', the great Dr. Jekyll had turned into Mr. Hyde. No matter what his actual words were, no matter how he really may have phrased it, we perceived his voice to say loud and clear:

> *"I am god. I have the right, the power, and the omniscience to perfectly dictate what Jay needs outside my care, outside my space, outside my practice. I have the prerogative to pull out. You, the very, very sick patient and the very, very tired care-taker, can fare for yourselves. I know you are vulnerable. I know your hands are tied.*

However, your position makes me even more powerful so you must walk the path I choose and die."

After all his care, after all his efforts, this oncologist ultimately did more harm to the patient than any other. To violate trust, to abandon the frail is to put the 'b-u-t' in the sentence.

Everything we heard before, everything we experienced prior, everything we believed about our care became void, null, non-existent. The violation became master, trumping all else.

"You must give Jay IV fluids at home," the oncologist warned.

"I don't think so, sir," I contended. "Jay takes fluids anytime I give them to him. You tell me how many ounces he needs a day, I will see that he gets it."

"There is no way you can do this," the oncologist preached. "We will insert a PIC line and you must be set-up for IVs or you can't take him home."

Home IVs were arranged. However, the message was devastating. "IV fluids will cost the family $2,000 a month," they said. "You must pay $500 upfront."

"That is highway robbery," I said. "You are telling us to pay $500 a quart for saline water worth $1.25?"

"Oh, we have to sterilize it and . . . .." they began.

"You can't defend that gouger's fee to me. You know it's criminal. So don't try. Save your breath," I argued. "It is just amazing to me that saline water will be the cost that breaks us."

"Okay, okay," I said in defeat, "it's not about me. It's about Jay. If hospice will pay for the IVs, let's change and go to hospice."

"If you go to hospice, they can't pay for the Temodar," they answered. "While in hospice, he can have no medication in his diagnosis."

"Great, that's just great. Here is my dilemma: I want to care for Jay in the best way possible. If I go with home health, I will pay $2000 a month for saline water. If I go with hospice, they won't allow him to take chemotherapy. And if they did, I would pay $3000 a month for it because they won't pay for it."

And we live in America! America cares for their veterans, their farmers, their contributors? Jay was all three. He fought for this country, he fed this country, and he worked until the day he was diagnosed. Now he is nothing but a throw-away?

"He will take Temodar," I said. "That is not in question. Hospice is a death sentence. We have no choice, but to go to home health. It is amazing that the system would gladly throw Jay into long-term care with the state eventually paying the expenses, but they won't support his wife who is eager to love him and care for him. It makes absolutely no sense."

When the ambulance arrived from the hospital bringing Jay home, we noticed his arms were covered with bruises. "What is this?" I asked.

"They couldn't get a PIC line in," they answered. "They worked hours on him. They inserted this IV to accommodate the fluids."

The next day, the home health nurse asked for Jay's fluid intake records. "With these numbers, why are we doing IV fluids?" she asked.

"Beats me," I said in defeat. "I told the doctor that Jay would drink the fluids for me. He wouldn't listen. That's the way it is in the medical world."

"I'll call the doctor and see if we can't do a few days trial without the IV fluids." The nurse responded.

Jay's fluid intake was more than satisfactory. We threw $500 worth of saline water in the trash.

Angels Among Us

The person-to-person connections doctors make with their patients are not just pleasant amenities but an integral part of medical care. (Abramson, 2005)

In his book, *Keeping Hope Alive*, Lewis Smedes states: *False hope can be worse than no hope at all.*

Jay and I understood this concept. We knew the bottomless pit of false hope. False hope is empty, barren, desolate. It is foreign to the true hope we held for Jay's recovery. This hope was born from the knowledge that Jay *would* recover, whether here in his earthly home or there in his heavenly home. This hope was guaranteed.

False hope was foreign to our true hope that Jay would continue to feel comfortable, enjoy his family and friends, and live until he died. This hope manifested itself daily as his team rallied around him, supported him, and loved him, ignoring the agenda set against him.

The false hope was our hope that someone in medicine would hear Jay's cry for mercy, that someone would see Jay for the man he was, and that someone would meet us at the emergency room door, wanting Jay to live the last few precious moments of his life with *real* comfort care, with *real* support services, with *real* understanding!

One man in white with invisible wings did break the chains of false hope one night. After feeling sick myself, after crying, after searching my soul about which emergency room to use *this time*, I finally just chose one.

I expected scorn. I expected a condescending manner. I expected nothing. However, after hearing our story, the emergency room doctor said, "I have been a doctor for many years. Please listen to what I have to say. You are not crazy. The system is!"

I couldn't believe my ears and I couldn't believe my eyes. This doctor talked to Jay, he x-rayed Jay, he gave him antibiotics for his cough, saying "Jay doesn't have a full-blown infection at this time, but I want him to have these antibiotics to protect him for the next few days."

The doctor explained that he couldn't see any food aspirated into Jay's lungs. "However, when it becomes difficult to swallow, aspiration is a possibility," he said. "A person can aspirate without coughing or showing discomfort, so the care-taker may not be aware."

What information, what relief, what comfort this man bestowed upon us. As we were leaving the emergency room to return home, the doctor called after us, "Just remember," he said, "you are not crazy. The system is!"

Home Health - Mickey Mouse Health Care

Those who preach about "how to die with dignity" only feign their expertise since they haven't been there. Too bad they can't discuss "how to live until you die", but maybe they haven't been there either. (Silliman, 2007)

Three people at home health were important to Jay. They included one rehabilitation therapist, Jay's first assigned nurse, and the gentleman who gave him his baths. Jay loved to see each of them come.

They visited with Jay and many times sneaked a little extra time for him. However, each time a crisis occurred, Jay's assigned nurse was off duty or busy with another patient.

We quickly learned that home health staff was mirror-images of the rest of the American healthcare system. They didn't listen, they knew everything, and they didn't back-track even if white was proven black.

The home health evaluative rehabilitation therapist tested Jay for services. She woke him from a nap and he was still a bit groggy. She tried to help him sit up in bed. She had her hand on his back and he leaned back toward her hand.

Looking over at the commode beside the bed, the therapist said, "I don't think you should put Jay on that commode. He can't sit up and he will push the whole thing over. It's not safe."

"Jay can and does sit up. You need to let him move around a little," I explained. "He's been asleep and is groggy. He has been doing very well. He sits on the edge of the bed with his feet dangling off the side all the time."

The therapist ignored me. She continued to push Jay and never allowed him to react on his own. She didn't listen and she left before her evaluation was completed.

That night, Jay woke me up rattling his bed. I looked up. He was sitting at the bottom of the bed with his legs off the sides. He was about ready to stand up.

"No, Jay, please don't get up, sweetheart."

"Why." he countered?

"I need to help you. I don't want you to fall."

The next morning I called home health. "You need to either tell the evaluating therapist to come back and reevaluate Jay or she needs to document my call in her records. She indicated that Jay couldn't sit up yesterday. She needs to know Jay pulled himself up with no assistance and sat on the side of the bed. If she reports that he can't sit, that is incorrect information. The rehab therapist won't know where to begin therapy."

When the rehab therapist arrived for Jay's first workout, she exclaimed, "Jay is doing much more than the report indicates. I wasn't prepared for this. I'll work with him today, but I'll need to readjust my plans."

"I called the office to tell the therapist to reevaluate Jay or to amend her report with the information that I was providing. Obviously, she discounted me," I said. Then under my breath I added, "After six months, healthcare still doesn't know the doctors missed their two-month mark. They still don't know that Jay isn't dead yet!"

"What did you say?" she asked.

"Oh, nothing," I answered. I knew that any further comment at this point was futile. The spider web of ignorance and blind-ear perforated home health also. Jay and I were alone. The battle was an ongoing struggle. That night a nightmare shattered my rest.

I was in the ocean. It was dark, murky. and cold. For some reason, I had huge fins on my feet. My hands were tied behind my back. I changed direction by turning, twisting my body. I could maneuver, but barely. It was slow and laborious. I swam here and there, searching.

Then I heard a loud, clear voice with megaphone sound. "Y-o-u are not doing it." It echoed. "Y-o-u are not doing it. You must retrieve the money now. If you want Jay to live, you must get it now. You must hurry." The voice echoed. Jay is dying. Hurry, Hurry, Hurry."

I worked harder, flapping my feet, arching and twisting my body, pushing, pushing - physically, emotionally, spiritually!

As always, when I woke up, sweat was streaming down my face. I was extremely fatigued, but I got up and walked over to Jay's bed. I watched him sleep. Then I leaned over and kissed his forehead. I turned and sat on the couch beside his bed and fell asleep.

Even though the nightmares were devastating, I knew they were my friend. They were my friend because they allowed me to express subconsciously what I could not express consciously. They were explosions of the fear, frustration, and rage that I was feeling, but for Jay's sake, for my sake, I suppressed daily. God, in His infinite wisdom, gave me nightmares for a way to cope, for a way out!

Away From the Deadly Zoo

I found that there is an authentic biology of hope Researchers are learning that a change in mind-set has the power to alter neurochemistry. (Groopman, 2004)

Jay and I stayed up almost all night. Then we would sleep until nine or ten o'clock in the morning. Jay loved to eat. He loved his breakfast the most, always eating it to the last bite. He ate two eggs, a piece of stone-ground whole wheat toast, and fruit yogurt. He drank freshly squeezed fruit and vegetable juice and plenty of water. After breakfast, we watched television, listened to Country Gospel music, or talked.

Sometimes Jay and I went to the mall. We always did something different. Some days we looked at shirts, other days we looked at toys; sometimes we raced the halls, sometimes we just watched people. I might even push Jay's wheelchair in and out of the women's lingerie department, light-heartedly teasing him about his protests.

Since home health rules hand-cuff patients to the home to be eligible for services, Jay and I couldn't leave the house unless we had a doctor appointment or some other official reason to be off the premises. However, we quickly learned how to pour life into our outings.

After our excursions, we usually went home and took a nap so we could wake up and get busy. Around seven each evening, we had a new surge of energy and our day began in earnest.

"Jay, would you like to read children's books together," I asked. "That would be like going to Nemo or The Toy Story. Reading these books will help you continue to read, they'll keep you mentally sharp."

Jay answered with his usual one-word, up-beat answer, "Sure," he said.

So we read them - the easy readers. We loved this time together. I would read a page. Then Jay would read a page. He loved reading about animals especially horses, dogs, and other farm animals.

His very favorite book, however, was about the relationship of a mother to her children - *"I'll Love You Forever" by Robert N. Munsch and Sheila McGraw.*

"I'll love you forever, I'll like you for always, As long as I'm living, My baby you'll be." Jay would read. Then he would smile. Later, when Jay was too sick to read, the family read to him. He still loved this story and listened intently. Many times when we finished the story and put the book down, we would detect a tear in the corner of his eye.

I believe this story touched Jay in two ways. First, one of his favorite things to say from the day I met him was: "My kids can do anything and they will still be my kids!" And, secondly, he was extremely close to his own mother. Family members were still calling him "Mama's Favorite" years after his mother died and when he was 78 years old.

Some people might say, "Man, I never want to be in that shape! If I get like that just put me away."

That's everyone's prerogative, but looking back, Jay was in the best shape ever. Jay never had any pretense, but at this moment, during this time in his life, his true personality emerged to the very surface of his being.

Jay had become candid and verbal with childlike innocence. With inhibitions gone, he was demonstrating to the world the sweet, generous, caring nature his family had always known and loved. So instead of wishing that we never reach that point in life, maybe it would be better if we wished for the same purity and honesty that Jay exuded at this time.

The most wonderful testimony, however, is that Jay dispelled the doctors' myths one more time. He was not like a patient suffering from Alzheimer disease, he had not pulled away from family and friends (he moved in closer), his personality had not escaped him and made him someone different. He was a thinking, evaluating, feeling, responding Jay.

Jay also put children's puzzles together. They were all 'man' appropriate, including big road equipment, cars, and exotic animals. He worked at them for hours. It kept his fingers nimble and his right hand working.

Then we did the hard stuff. We were so far ahead of home health in physical therapy; we couldn't look back and see them in our dust. Medicare dictates that home health can't work with the patient, but must teach the care-taker how to do physical therapy. So we basically put them out "on the back porch" and designed Jay's rehab program ourselves.

One home health therapist shared with me, "You are so far ahead of what I can do for you. You need to just dismiss us and forge ahead."

So we did. I had Jay on a regular workout regimen. He went from one piece of equipment to another, working out at least thirty minutes at a time. We loved doing it together. He was a trouper and worked extremely hard at it. Jay never stopped being congenial, helpful, and willing. Ever!

Don, Rose's husband, mounted straps on the ceiling above the treadmill. We bought a climber's vest that had straps over the shoulders and around the legs. This attached to the straps hanging from the ceiling. If Jay's feet came out from under him, he didn't fall. He would be sitting in the climber's vest, swinging in the air. Jay walked the treadmill three to five minutes at a time this way.

Next, Jay moved to the recumbent bike. He would ride his bike up to fifteen minutes at a time. I sat beside him and talked with him. If one of his feet slipped off the pedal, I put it back on. We laughed. I told him how strong and able he was. He loved his bike and 'owned it' with pride. He beamed when I bragged to others about his accomplishments on the bike.

The last equipment was Jay's favorite. It was a sit-up chair. He loved swinging back in an arch. He told me it felt good.

Sometimes I would beg him to 'come back up' because I didn't want the blood to rush to his head. He bounced back and forth on the chair and laughed. He always wanted to sit in the chair, and was never ready to get out of it.

There was only one minor mishap in Jay's exercise program. One day as I was helping Jay from his wheelchair to the exercise bike, we missed the seat of the bike.

When I realized we were a couple of inches below the seat, I didn't have the strength to lift Jay back up to that level. And in that position, his legs were not strong enough to push him back up either. So he slid slowly, easily to the floor. He couldn't get up. I couldn't lift him.

"It's okay, Jay," I said. "I'll find a way." Jay didn't get excited. He didn't complain. He accepted his plight, waiting there on the floor quietly, patiently in true Jay fashion. I scanned the room, looking for help. Then I saw the chair lift his brother, Bill, bought for him.

I pulled it over to Jay and raised the foot rest about three or four inches. I pulled Jay up so his torso was on the foot rest. I continued to electronically raise the chair until I could get my arms under his. Then with my help, he stood up. Jay wasn't hurt and we were elated. "What did I tell you, Sweetheart, we're a team! Praise, God!" We stood there a moment, holding each other, laughing. Then we cried.

When we brought Jay home from the neighboring hospital, I decided we should live in our basement. We have a walk-out basement with a family room as large as four rooms upstairs. The family room has a complete mini-kitchen and is accessible to the bathroom, laundry room, and exercise room. My office is also nearby with a computer online.

We put Jay's hospital bed next to the door. When guests arrived, he was right there. He saw every guest arrive and told them goodbye when they left, yelling "come back" as they exited the door. One of his favorite guests was our pastor.

Jay loved being in the mainstream and we loved it too. I never left his side. I slept on the couch three feet from his bed and with everything at our fingertips, it couldn't have been better. It was a great set-up.

Delbert hauled his golf cart to our backdoor from Western Kansas. The golf cart provided a way out over the back yard when it rained. Mickey came and helped maintain equipment.

With all the exercising and Jay's love for water therapy, I decided he might enjoy a jet tub. We were going to install one in the exercise room anyway, but never got around to it. When I told Rhonda that we were going to install a jet-tub, she warned, "Mom, be careful. You need to check with the doctor regarding Jay's medication and his condition before you put him in a jet tub."

So I talked with Jay's home health nurse. She said she didn't see a problem with it, but would share the idea with others. After the home health nurses discussed it, they gave us a green light, saying it was a good idea and it would help circulation.

Don installed the tub. I helped Jay get into his swimming trunks. Then Rose and Don helped me give him his first jet tub experience. After about ten minutes, Rose said, "Mom, I think we better take Jay out. He is pink to the tip of his toes."

We helped Jay out of the tub and into bed. As I was straightening up around the bed, Jay's eyes began to blink, he began to grind his teeth, his face began to pulsate. He was having a seizure.

I cupped his face between my hands, trying to stop the process. I prayed out loud, "Oh, God, please, not this. Please." The seizure stopped.

My hands were still cupped on Jay's cheeks and I was bending over him with fear in my eyes and tears running down my face.

Jay looked up at me with wide-eyed surprise. He studied my face for a moment. Then with the deepest concern and care, he said, "You know what? . . . I am really getting worried about you!"

Amazing! The man who was fighting for his life, the man who had every reason to be self-absorbed, the man who was suppose to be detached, was worried about his wife.

I laughed with relief and said, "And I am really getting worried about you too!"

The home health nurse wanted the doctor to start Jay on an anti-seizure medication. However, after she called the doctor, he returned the call to me.

"I wasn't there so I can't tell you exactly what happened," he said. "However, I can give you the physiology of it. If you or I had a tendency to seize and we were in a jet tub for ten minutes, we would seize."

"That's all I needed to know, doctor," I said. "We will not go there again."

After I hung up the phone, it hit me like a brick. Jay had his two other seizures while he was in water therapy. No one told me that warm, moving water was dangerous for Jay.

The internist had ordered the water therapy. Why didn't he know? I talked to the emergency room doctor about Jay's water therapy. Why didn't he know? I asked home health about the jet tub. Why didn't they know?

Jay suffered again because a disjointed, simple-minded, system was not patient focused. Jay and I were truly alone in a bleak world.

Campaigning for Retreat

I tell my patients that the more aggressive the disease, the more aggressive the treatment," Nimer said, And because it is a "bad disease," the doctor should increase his efforts rather than retreat. Sometimes a bad disease can be cured. (Groopman, 2007)

Jay grimaced. "What's the matter?" I asked.

"My elbow," he answered. "It hurts."

I looked at his elbow. It was swollen and red. Even though it was late evening, I called home health. I explained about Jay's elbow and said I was concerned. He hadn't been hurt, there were no breaks in the skin, and I couldn't think of a reason for the swelling.

"Well," came the reply, "you don't want to take him out tonight, do you?"

"If it's necessary, I certainly do," I snapped. "That's why I'm calling. You should know what I need to do."

*Dr. Stephen Nimer, hematologist who specializes in leukemia, lymphoma, and other malignant disorders of the bone marrow.(Groopman, 2007)

"I can't see any reason why it would be that urgent," the home health nurse said. "Why don't you wait until tomorrow and tell your assigned nurse?"

So reluctantly, I waited until morning. When Jay's nurse arrived, I showed her his elbow. "It looks like gout," she said. "I'll call the doctor this morning."

I relaxed some. I had heard about gout and didn't think it would be big problem. We went on with our schedule the next couple of days. Then at 3:50 p.m. the doctor's nurse called. "Can you have Jay here in ten minutes?" she asked.

"No," I answered. "I'm here alone with Jay. It would take me ten minutes to pull the car around and get Jay in it. Then it would take me time to drive to the clinic. Can you wait just ten or fifteen minutes longer?"

"No," she said. "We are closing. Just come in tomorrow morning." She didn't indicate that we might have a problem on our hands. She didn't suggest I take Jay to the emergency room.

The next morning, Jay was lethargic. He stared into space and I couldn't get him to respond to me. Terrified, I called 911. The ambulance arrived. "Don't take him to Breech Medical Center," I instructed. "Take him to Darnel-Crest Hospital."

They put Jay in the ambulance and were ready to go. Then one of the EMTs took the time to get out of the ambulance, walk back to the door and ask, "If he quits breathing, do you want us to resuscitate him?"

"Absolutely," I ordered! "Why do you think I called you? Go! Get on the road, now."

The ambulance had just arrived at the hospital when I got there. I had to drive the speed limit and stop for lights. I couldn't imagine what took the ambulance so long. I went into the emergency room to find Jay.

The emergency crew was just standing there, discussing Jay's blood pressure. No one was moving. No one was doing anything. "His blood pressure is so low; it won't even register," they said. "It has dropped out of sight."

The minute I entered the room, the full-court press began. One nurse walked over beside me. She took hold of my arms and applied light pressure. She said, "Think about it before you resuscitate him. Think about what you are doing to him. Think about *quality* of life."

The crew standing over Jay turned to me and said, "Do you want him resuscitated? He is barely breathing."

"Yes, resuscitate him," I answered.

"Do you realize that if we insert a respirator that he could have a heart attack?" they argued.

"We'll face that if it happens. Resuscitate him!" I demanded louder.

The voice beside me continued, "Sometimes it is too hard for some people to let go. You need to check with other family members about resuscitating him. You may make him a vegetable!"

"Do you realize," the emergency crew continued to argue, "that if we insert the respirator, you may not be able to remove it?"

"Put it in!" I screamed.

I was becoming faint. I couldn't think. I was in a room of antagonists. They wanted Jay to die. They didn't want to bother with him. They didn't know him. They didn't care.

I started for the door. "Rose should be in the waiting room," I thought. "I have to find her!" The nurse hanging at my arm followed me out the door and down the hall, chattering, badgering, pushing for me to "let Jay go."

Rose was there. "Thank you, Lord," I said. Then I cried, "They are trying to get *me* to kill Jay. The nurse is standing beside me, holding my arms, pressuring me."

Rose and I went through the double doors to return to Jay's side. The nurse was waiting for us on the other side. "Have you decided what you are going to do?" she asked.

"Out of our face," Rose demanded. "We don't have enough information at this time to make a decision like that. Tests indicate his tumor is smaller and has stabilized. It may be his elbow."

"Well," the nurse replied, "I've never heard of an elbow doing that."

The hospitalist burst through the door. "Thank you," he said, "for inserting the respirator. My guess is this is septic shock from the elbow. We need to get his blood pressure elevated stat!" He continued to bark orders. The crew came alive, jumping into action.

"I want him in the Intensive Care Unit (ICU) as quickly as possible," he said. "Let's move it."

Moments after the hospitalist arrived, Jay was on his way to ICU. We followed and went to the waiting room. When the doctor came to visit with us, he said, "The tumor is smaller and stabilized. He is in septic shock. The shock was most likely caused by his infected elbow. He should pull through okay. We'll do everything we can."

"The home health nurse told us his elbow looked like gout," I said.

"It does," the doctor answered, "but gout can become infected. The ICU nurses will call you back in a few minutes. They'll have some questions for you. I am leaving on vacation tomorrow so I won't be seeing you again. The other doctors on duty will take good care of you."

I stayed in ICU with Jay. He began to respond. They successfully removed the respirator. He was improving, but everything was not okay. I became uneasy, watching the doctors, nurses, and guests put on gowns, masks, and gloves before entering the room next to Jay's.

I thought, "Jay has a compromised immune system. Why would they chance putting him next door to someone with an infectious disease? What if it is a staph infection and a nurse fails to wash her hands?"

Then it happened. The respiratory nurse came into Jay's room and she didn't wash her hands. As she came toward Jay, I lunged over his bed, putting my hands on him for protection.

"Don't touch him," I demanded.

"Why?" she asked in surprise.

"Because you didn't wash your hands," I accused.

"I washed them in the other room," she answered.

"The sign right here, in Jay's room, right in front of your eyes reads: *Wash Your Hands When Entering This Room and Wash Your Hands When Leaving This Room.* You did not wash your hands when you entered."

Jay began to cry. The hall nurse came into the room, "What's the matter?" she asked.

"The nurse just came from the room next door and didn't wash her hands. Jay has a compromised immune system from chemotherapy. Why is he next door to a patient with an infectious disease anyway?" I asked.

"I'll be back in just one minute," she said and flew out of the room.

She returned with a moving crew. "There is a room on the other side of ICU," she said. "We are moving Jay over there stat."

Angels Among Us

A single rose can be my garden . . . . A single friend, my world.
(Leo Buscaglia)

After the hospitalist rescued Jay from the emergency room at Darnel Crest Hospital, he said he would return soon to update us on Jay's condition. As we sat waiting, I began to fear. Visions of fifteen years ago flooded my head. Dad was in Darnel-Crest then.

Dad was active, traveling around the country with a friend. He was 81. Since Dad was in excellent health, this was the first time he was admitted to this hospital. The doctor determined that he had a kinked intestine and Dad underwent surgery.

Following surgery, they took him to ICU as was customary. When I went in to see him, a nurse met me at the door.

"What do you want do to in case of a Code Blue," she demanded.

Surprised, I said, "Everything. He's post-operative. Do everything for him that you would do for anyone else just out of surgery."

"Everything," she responded with emotion. "Do you know what everything is?"

"I don't care what everything is," I demanded.

"How old is he?" she queried.

"What difference does it make how old he is? He is my father." I demanded. And the confrontation began . . . .

Now fifteen years later, we were starting all over again? Was this the same nurse in the emergency room or was it hospital protocol? I wondered.

When the hospitalist returned and told us the nurses would

be calling me, I didn't know that I was about to meet someone dressed in white with invisible wings. However, when the nurses called my name and I went to meet them, they reached out to me and said:

"We just love your husband. He is so sweet. And we know that he is back, because he does everything we ask him to do."

Their words, their smiles, their touches were more than I could bear. I began to sob. They put their arms around me. The room became warm and my muscles relaxed. I felt I could sleep once again.

The nurses assured me they would be with Jay throughout the night. They promised they would call if he needed me. I trusted them. Jay was with friends. I went to the ICU waiting room, curled up on the couch, and slept like a baby.

Closed Minds, Closed Possibilities

There are in fact two things, science and opinion; the former begets knowledge, the later ignorance. (Hippocrates)

Jay recovered from sepsis enough to move to a regular hospital room. I slept on a cot beside his bed. He had developed a bronchial condition so they put him on breathing treatments. Everything was going well until the *Dancer* came into the room.

The one personality Jay was most likely to shy away from was the 'look at me personality.' This personality is constantly on show, being funny, making jokes, chattering for attention.

The dancing nurse-aide pranced around Jay's bed, giggly and animated. Occasionally, her medical partner gave a chuckle, providing incentive for her act. The dancer took Jay's Depends off, leaving him exposed to the room. Jay's expression became serious, aptly displaying his discomfort. I thought about intervening, but decided the uproar may upset him even more. So I just tried to temper the situation.

Giggling continuously, the aide grabbed a small square cloth and placed it over Jay's private area. Then she turned to her partner, batted her eyes, tittered as she spoke to Jay in baby-talk, "There, there," she said, "we don't want you to wee wee on us."

I had never seen Jay so visibly upset. He was enraged! I tried to calm him in my own appalled sense. However, he couldn't calm down. Just as the dancer left the room, the respiratory nurse entered. She put the treatment mask on Jay's face.

Jay immediately grabbed the mask off his face and threw it across the room. The respiratory nurse was frightened. She ran into the hall and reported it to the head nurse. The head nurse came, flying into the room, and I explained what had happened.

"Well," she responded, "It is about seven o'clock in the evening. Jay is suffering from Sundowners."

"Sundowners," I questioned, "what is that? He doesn't have Sundowners. He's angry!"

"Well," the nurse countered, "I have been in this business a long time and I know. Sundowners is when a brain tumor patient or Alzheimer's patient becomes unruly, disoriented, and agitated in the evening hours."

"The evening hours are our best time of the day. He doesn't have Sundowners. He's mad!" I repeated with emphasis.

She left the room knowing what she knew - it was Sundowners. I remained knowing what I knew - it wasn't.

The next day a nurse came to Jay's door. She looked familiar, but I couldn't place where I had seen her. "Haven't I seen you somewhere before?" I asked.

"We might have met somewhere before," she answered. She spoke in a sing/song manner and had a bounce in her step. When she pushed her way into the room, she walked over to Jay's bed. I walked on the other side instinctively wanting to protect him.

"I was the nurse in the emergency room. I hope I didn't offend you," she confessed.

"Yes. You did," I emphasized. "You harassed me."

"Well," she continued, "that's a hard decision to make."

"No, it wasn't and isn't," I said as I started to cry. "My mind was made up. I knew what I wanted to do. You tried to change my mind. You harassed me."

She left the room and I went into the hall. I asked the nurse on duty for her name. "She didn't come to Jay's room to apologize," I stated. "She came to defend her position."

Finally, the day arrived. Jay and I could retreat from the war-zone once again. Jay was going home. The hospitalist, filling in for the doctor on vacation, came into the room to dismiss him.

Standing at the foot of Jay's bed he said, "Jay will not be doing what he was doing before he came into the hospital. He will not be able to exercise again."

"That is your opinion, doctor," I said. "However, Jay is willing and I am determined, so we will just have to wait and see."

"I mean *EVER*," he pushed.

"Yes," I said. "I'll have to rehabilitate him as always after leaving the hospital and we will have to wean him off the increased Decadron you put him on. But don't be surprised at what we can accomplish."

The gentleman seethed disgust and contempt. He started to leave the room.

"By the way," I asked, "will you prescribe a respirator so we can continue breathing treatments at home?"

"He doesn't need the treatments anymore," he growled. Then he turned to leave the room.

Rose followed him. "We want you to prescribe a respirator for Jay," she said. "I have one for my little girls. The doctor told me to never abruptly stop treatment. Jay has been on three treatments a day for ten days. How can you just stop the treatments cold-turkey?"

The doctor prescribed a respirator.

Three days after we returned home from Darnel-Crest hospital, Jay said, "I want to go to the exercise room."

"What do you want to do there," I asked?

"I want to ride my bike," he said.

"Do you think you can?" I questioned.

"Why can't I?" he responded.

"It beats the pudding out of me." I said. Let's go for it."

Jay rode his recumbent bike and we had a great time.

Later Jay and I had a conversation that resurfaced from time to time. I didn't like this conversation. My distaste wasn't because we talked about our deaths; it was because the conversation demonstrated the power doctors have over their patients, the impact their words have on the healing process.

Nine months after the doctors told Jay he would be dead, he was alive continuing to carry those meaningless words in his head.

"I'm getting really old," Jay said. "I am dying, you know."

"You said you were young just a few months ago, Jay. So you are only a few months older now," I reminded him. "And, yes, I know you are dying. I am dying too. We just don't know when."

"Yes, we do," he corrected me. "I am going to die in two months."

"Jay, sweetheart, the doctors missed it. They were wrong. They said that last April, remember? This is Christmas. April was nine months ago. Two months passed a long time ago. The doctors don't know when we will die; only God knows that."

"Oh, yes," Jay mused. "Only God knows. We will live 'til we die, right? The doctors really don't know."

"You're right," I said. "Hey, remember what Rhonda told us to do when we get blue? If we get blue, we need to sing ha, ha, ha, ho, ho, ho, hee, hee, hee."

Then we began the ritual. Ha, ha, ha, ho, ho, ho, hee, hee, hee. We did this until we both broke out in laughter. "I love you, Jay, more than you will ever know. Thank you for being you."

Our joy was short-lived because Jay's home health nurse resigned from her job for a better position in an institution. Since home health had a staff shortage, they scheduled a hospice nurse to come to our home.

No one had to tell me she was from hospice. I knew it immediately. We tangled from the first moment. She was condescending, continually telling me that I needed to face reality. That night I woke up screaming. I had a horrible nightmare. It was real. It was terrifying.

Everything was pitch black. I yelled and yelled, but my voice just echoed back at me. "Help, Help," I screamed! "My husband is dying. Please help us. Please help us. P-L-E-A-S-E!

No one would come. No one would assist me. Someone was there though because voices began to emerge and retreat, laughing, mocking, threatening. "Quit hurting Jay. Quit trying to save him. Quit taking our time. He is dying. He is dying.

You just need to shut up and let him goooooooo."

The next day, I called home health. "Why did you send a hospice nurse to see Jay?" I asked. "I told you to never send a hospice nurse to our home."

"We are short staffed," was the reply. "We trade nurses back and forth."

"No, you don't send hospice to our home. I don't have to sit and listen to someone in my own home reprimand me for my beliefs. Don't *EVER* do that again! That is final."

I walked over to Jay's bed. "Hi, sweetheart," I cooed. "Do you need me to climb in bed with you? Do you want me to hold you?"

"Yes," he said, "I would like that."

I put on a Country Gospel CD, scooted Jay over a little and climbed into the hospital bed. I wrapped my arms tightly around his chest, kissed him on the neck, and whispered 'I love you' in his ear.

Tears flooded my eyes and I prayed, "Dear Lord, if you are taking Jay, please help me to savor this moment. Help me to feel this feeling over and over again after he is gone. Be with us, Lord, I pray."

It was time for a change. Jay and I designed, initiated, and carried out his daily rehabilitation. We created his nutritional program. He didn't have a home health nurse anymore. Jay suffered a seizure because they didn't guide us on medical care. They were more trouble than they were worth.

However, the final blows were in the evaluative therapist progress report and the oncologist's official abandonment. When the evaluative therapist returned to establish Jay's progress, his report was unbelievable. "We can't help you anymore," he said. "Jay has not shown any improvement."

"What do you mean, he hasn't shown improvement? He walks the treadmill, rides his bike, and works the sit-up chair. When he came home from the hospital he could just sit up."

"Well," he said, "he doesn't sit up in bed any differently than he did. We have rules that we must follow."

"That is the most idiotic thing I have ever heard. Why don't you look at the whole person. You are no help anyway," I ranted. "You need to leave."

The oncologist told home health that he was not the doctor on call anymore. I talked with him on the telephone, "Why are you deserting us?" I asked.

"I told you that I couldn't be your doctor when you left the hospital here. I stayed with you for that last chemotherapy round. Everyone dies sometime and Jay's medicine will kill him before the cancer does. J.R. Cancer Center will no longer offer consultation either," he said.

Everyone was gone again. It was just Jay, the cancer and I. The darkness enveloped me. My mouth became dry. My skin became pasty. I felt chills crawling up my back.

I hung up the telephone and cried: "And . . and. . .and so *what if* the treatment kills him before the cancer - - - and *what if it doesn't* kill him before the cancer? What if it *cures* him? Doctors' negligence allowed Jay to have sepsis, the treatment just *tried* to give it to him."

My voice became stronger. I was yelling in a whisper so Jay couldn't hear me: "I told them he had a swollen elbow; home health told them he had a swollen elbow. Did anyone answer our call for help? No! No! They waited four days!

"Do you hear me? Do you hear me? It took four days for them to answer my call. . . . . And you say you do no harm? Yes you do! Yes you do! You do harm through your arrogance! You do harm through your negligence! You do harm through your greed and your apathy!

"Jay suffered sepsis because of *YOU!*" Then my voice trailed off: "Do you hear me? Do you hear me?" I sobbed.

The Calm Before the Storm

We should never shy away from the challenges that face us out of fear of failure or an unwillingness to battle the odds. We should confront our problems head on, and make no excuses. (Maynard, 2005)

Jay was happy at home. He didn't have pain. He didn't have seizures. I only gave him an occasional aspirin, mainly to calm him and help him sleep. When Rose and her family came to visit, several things were cemented regulars.

When they arrived, Rose would always go straight to Jay's bed or his wheelchair or to wherever he was and begin singing, *"Amazing grace, how sweet the sound that saved a wretch like me! I once was lost, but now am found, was blind, but now I see."*

Jay always immediately joined the one-person chorus, humming the tune to the top of his lungs. We always commended him for his wonderful singing and asked him to do it again.

Many times we ordered pizza. Jay had always had his supper because I was very particular about his diet. However, when the pizza arrived, Jay would yell, "Where's mine!" We would laugh at the expected outburst and take him a piece to enjoy.

After leaving home health, I bought a wheelchair accessible van. When I showed Jay a picture of the van on the internet, he was very excited, "We need to sell the pickup," he said.

"Yup, Jay," I agreed. "You still know the business, don't you? You never fail me, ever. You are a good man."

After the van arrived, Jay and I never stayed home. Many times I cried with joy about how mobile and happy we were. However, I was angry deep down inside because we had wasted such precious, precious time with the home health tom-foolery. We were finally doing what Jay wanted to do - live until he died!

We had enrolled Jay in out-patient physical therapy to complement what we were doing at home. Two men worked with him at Tallgrass Immediate Care facility.

Jay worked his heart out for them. He loved it.

Every morning, Jay would ask, "Where are we going today?"

I would tell him if we had an appointment or physical therapy and, if not, I would ask, "I don't know. Where would you like to go today?" Then we would go to the mall or to Gage Park to see the flowers or watch the children play. One of our favorite pastimes was to go to Sonic for a breakfast burrito. Jay could eat the burrito easily so I relinquished his diet for these occasional outings.

One day when we were headed to Sonic, our pastor came for his weekly visit. He jumped in the van and went along with us, and we had a great time. Jay and I had breakfast burritos; Pastor had a sundae.

Another day was especially good for Jay. He went to physical therapy and stood between the bars for the therapists. They gave him a tool to hang above his bed to work his arms back and forth.

When we went home, he worked and worked this apparatus. He hummed one song after another as he worked.

"You're really feeling good today," I remarked. "I'm so glad you are enjoying yourself."

I was naïve. I thought Jay was improving; I didn't realize we were in the final days before the last episode.

The Decency Mirage

It is healthy and beneficial to invest your ego in healing your patient's disease. But when your ego overshadows the goal, there lies danger. (Groopman, 2007)

We visited a Kansas City oncologist who was recommended to us. Before he came into the room, I warned the nurse that I was tired of doomsday predictions. "Jay has already outlived all of the earlier predictions and he doesn't need to hear more lies," I said.

When the doctor came in, he sat down in front of Jay. "Well," he said, "does Jay still enjoy life?"

Jay sat up straight in his wheelchair. He spoke with power and emphasis. His tone questioned the question. "Well, I guess I do!" he exclaimed.

The doctor half-smiled, looked at me, and said, "I guess that answers that." Then he looked back at Jay and said, "I was a farm boy once. Did you drive a *black* John Deere?"

Jay didn't answer, but looked at the doctor like he was crazy. When the doctor left the room, Jay turned to Rose and me and said, "These dicks don't have a clue!"

"What color is a John Deere?" Rose asked.

"Green," Jay said as if Rose were the crazy one now.

"What color is the deer on the John Deere tractor?" Rose continued to quiz.

"Yellow," Jay said looking at her in disbelief.

"Is it yellow?" I asked.

"Mom," Rose reprimanded, "yes, it's yellow. We had a John Deere tractor. Don't you remember?"

"I remember having a John Deere, but I don't remember a yellow deer on it," I said.

When I talked with the doctor later, I asked him about his John Deere question. "If you were testing Jay to see what he knows," I said, "you didn't wait for the punch line. He said you dicks don't have a clue."

The doctor smiled. "I was just teasing him," he said, "I wasn't trying to find out anything."

Then I asked the doctor about his opinions regarding treatment. "We have ordered bone marrow transplants to save patients," he said.

So Jay and I began to travel the fifty miles to Kansas City to see the doctor.

The Kansas City doctor ordered an MRI. When he received the results, he said, "The MRI indicated some enhanced areas in the brain. That could mean something or it may mean nothing. Jay can continue to take Temodar and I will order another MRI in a couple of months."

We returned home, but time was short . . . .

It was sudden. I called Rose. "Please come over. I think Jay is going into septic shock again. I don't want to take him to Darnel-Crest again. I guess I'll have to take him to Breech Medical Center. Oh, please just hurry."

The emergency room doctor was someone I knew. I had met him and his family at the local tennis club. He gave me a hug and worked diligently with Jay. After they stabilized Jay, they took him to the ward upstairs. The hospitalist called Rose and I into her office.

"The brain tumor is advancing," she said. "Have you ever thought about quality of life as you work to save him? He is dying."

"Who gets to choose what quality of life is to whom?" I asked. "Jay and I have neither one ever been a doctor. If you or your colleagues wouldn't have quality of life because you could no longer prescribe medicine, do surgery, or deliver babies, that's your hang-up. Don't apply your standards to us. We enjoy the simple life. We love each other."

"Do you want me to call in an oncologist for a second opinion?" She asked.

"No. You said that Jay has a bronchial condition. Treat the bronchial condition. Get him well enough that I can take him to Kansas City to his oncologist."

"I have already put in a request for an oncologist to come see him," she admitted.

"Then you had better cancel it," I warned. "No oncologist here is to see Jay."

"I don't know if I can retract it," she said.

"Retract it," I said. "You have no choice."

I was standing in the room beside Jay when the oncologist and his nurse came to Jay's bed side. He exposed his arrogance immediately, "I hear you wanted a second opinion," he said.

"No," I answered emphatically. "I don't want your . . . . .!"

"I am going to tell you the truth," he continued without listening to me. "I don't lie to my patients."

"We have heard all your truth we can stand," I countered. "We don't want to hear . . . . ."

"Did you know your doctor is lying to you?" he continued without pause. "Jay's tumor is advancing. He is dying. I don't lie to my patients. Jay should be in a study. The Temodar is not working anymore. I just don't have a study for him."

"Please listen to . . . . ."

The doctor walked out the door and started down the hall. I followed him and he continued talking, "I am going to call your oncologist. I'm going to tell him what I think of him!"

As the doctor disappeared down the hall, I turned to his nurse who stood at my side. "I really dislike these arrogant doctors," I said.

"I didn't think this oncologist was arrogant," she replied.

"Really," I asked? "You tell me what it was then. He gave me his opinion when I told him I didn't want it. He didn't let me finish a sentence. And he walked off when I was still talking to him."

The nurse thought a moment. "Yes," she said. "I guess that is arrogant."

The next day Rose and I went to see the hospitalist. "Jay is hungry. We want you to bring him some food. Every time he is in the hospital, he loses ground. You don't feed him, you don't exercise him, you stop his chemotherapy, you stop his thyroid medication."

"We want to give him a swallow test before we let him eat anything," she said.

"When will you do that?" Rose asked.

"In a couple of days," she replied.

"That is not soon enough," Rose argued. "He's hungry now.

You need to move the test-time up or give him some nutrients."

The hospitalist left the room. When she returned, she asked, "Do you want to go to a hospital in Kansas City so Jay's oncologist can work with you?"

"Yes," I answered. "Are they putting him in a good hospital? When will we go?"

"The ambulance will be here this afternoon," she said.

I wrote down the directions to the hospital and quickly made arrangements to go home and pick up some supplies. When I returned to the hospital, the nurse said, "Jay left for Kansas City approximately ten minutes ago."

"How was he doing?" I asked.

"We gave him some Ativan to calm him down," she said.

"Why did you do that?" I countered. "I forbade you to give him Ativan and you did it anyway? It will put him out. It will cause sleep apnea. Why did you do that?"

"We just gave a small dose," she argued.

"You were not to give Jay Ativan. Period. Do you not hear me? Ativan was a 'no give' medication. *No give!* Jay will be out for the next eight hours! If they don't watch him closely, he could quit breathing!"

Preparing the bed in Death Valley

. . . what appeared to be a rational form of thinking was actually irrational when applied to a patient's needs and goals, and might reflect the emotional state of the oncologist more than the clinical needs of the patient. (Groopman, 2007)

Jay was admitted to the Euthan Research Center in Kansas City. I was shocked at the casual attitude. His doctor didn't come to the room. No specialists came to the room. No one came to his room. It was as if Jay was admitted with the common cold - no big deal.

Jay was incoherent due to the dose of Ativan Breech Medical Center staff gave him. The nurse on duty at Euthan joined me in my concerns and watched Jay very closely.

They scheduled Jay for a swallow test to see if he was swallowing into his stomach, and refused to give him nutrients until the test was completed.

Meanwhile two rehabilitation therapists came to his room in response to my request. I had asked for them to do range of motion to help keep Jay mobile.

They walked into the room without even looking over at Jay. One said to the other, "He's a glio end-stage!" Then they walked over to the bed and helped him get up, without saying a word to him. Then they pivoted him around so he could sit in the chair beside his bed.

"What are you doing?" I asked. "Jay has not sat up for five days. I wanted you to do range of motion."

"We will just leave him here for a few minutes," they said. Then they left.

I sat and visited with Jay. The minutes passed. After an hour, Jay began to grimace. He said he was uncomfortable. I rang the nurse's station. "Yes," a voice said.

"Jay is uncomfortable and needs to be put back in bed," I said.

"I'll tell the nurse when she returns," the person answered.

Thirty more minutes elapsed. Jay was crying. I made two more calls to the nurses' station. "Jay has sat in this chair for one hour and thirty minutes," I said. "They will be coming to get him for the swallow test soon. He is in distress. P-l-e-a-s-e send someone to help me put him back to bed."

Rose called me on the telephone. "Hi, Mom how is everything?" she said.

I started to cry. "Jay has been sitting in a chair for over an hour. I have called the nurses' station three times. I'm going to put Jay back in bed by myself."

"Don't do that, Mom," Rose said. "I'm about five minutes away from the hospital. Wait until I get there. We can put him to bed together."

Before our conversation was completed, they came to take Jay for his swallow test. The test results were positive. Jay was swallowing into his stomach so he could begin to take some foods by mouth.

Our granddaughter said, "See. Grandpa, I told you that you

could do it."

Jay smiled, "Yep, I sure did," he responded with pride.

As we were returning to Jay's room, the rehabilitation therapist walked up to us and said, "Well, who put the patient back to bed?"

Rose moved closer to her face, pointed at her, and said, "It certainly wasn't you!" Rose and the therapist continued their heated conversation while we went back into the room.

Jay was getting very hungry. He cried. "My stomach hurts," he said. "Can I just have an apple?"

Rose began rubbing his stomach and assured him that we would get him some food. We were talking with him about what he wanted to order when the doctor walked into the room.

"Jay is hungry," I said. "He said his stomach is hurting. You need to give him some nutrition. He has only had sugar water in his IV. He has received no nutritional support for over a week."

The doctor put his pointing finger in the air and motioned for me to come with him into the hall. Then he yelled at me in a whisper, "You don't get it! Jay is seventy-eight years old. He is dying, dying, dying!"

"You don't get it," I screamed back. "He is hungry, hungry, hungry. He is asking for food. What are you going to do about it?"

"Nothing," he answered!

"Something," I said. "You surely have a nutrient bag you can hang. My husband needs nutrition."

"I have a nutrient bag that I can hang," he retorted, "but I am not hanging a $1000 bag of nutrients!"

"What's next then? You *will* do something," I demanded.

"I can stick a feeding tube down his nose," he threatened.

"Then do it!" I yelled.

The doctor huffed into Jay's room and stood beside his bed. Jay was crying. "Do you want a feeding tube down your nose," the doctor demanded.

Jay looked up at the doctor. His face was full of emotion. It was as if the beggar were soliciting the king. Jay's eyes said he knew this was the doctor and the doctor was the one who would help him. "Yes," he answered emphatically!

I became nauseated. I saw Jay's hope in a doctor who wanted to kill him. "I will never, never, get that look out of my head." I thought. "Jay thinks the doctor wants to help him, to feed him, but I know the doctor just wants him dead!"

The doctor became very angry. He made a quick turn for the door and spoke with deep contempt as he left, "I guess I'll have to do it then!"

They didn't take Jay to radiology. They didn't take any precautions. They tried inserting the feeding tube in the hospital bed. Three times they inserted it into the wrong place. Three times they attempted to reinsert it. Jay was never the same again.

When they completed their barbaric act, they taped the feeding tube on the tip of Jay's nose. The tape was blocking his eye-sight. He couldn't see around it.

"We can do intricate brain surgery and we can separate Siamese twins, but we can't figure a better way to anchor the feeding tube," I questioned.

"We can't change it now," they responded. "If we mess with it, we could pull it out."

"Well," I said, "the first thing Jay is going to do is pull it out. Anyone would do that. When he wakes up from a nap, he will reach for that tape."

That night around 11:00 p.m., Jay pulled the feeding tube out of his nose. Not one drop of nutrients had entered the tube. He had suffered for nothing.

The nurse on duty was one of those with invisible wings and I said to her, "They aren't going to do that to Jay again. Please call the doctor tonight and give him this message for me:

"You will order the nutrient bag tonight and you will hang it by morning. If you don't, I will call Jim Ryan and Sam Brownback, my Kansas U. S. Senator and Congressman tomorrow. I will tell them that you are withholding resources from my husband. Period."

The nurse did as I requested and the bag of nutrients was at Jay's bedside the next morning. However, Jay was now very, very ill. He coughed all through the night. The nurse worked with him diligently. However, his oxygen level kept dropping.

When the next oncologist came into Jay's room, I wasted no

time in saying what I had to say. "You practice euthanasia here," I said.

"No, we don't," he answered.

"Yes, you do," I quickly countered.

"My husband was asking for food yesterday and you were not going to give it to him. Do you hear me? My *husband* was asking for food; I wasn't asking for it; *he was!*"

"There is one thing that you need to know about me," I continued. "I do not believe in abortion. I do not believe in euthanasia! My husband fought for this country. He fed this country, and he worked until the day he was diagnosed. And you will return those resources to him!"

After the doctor left this conversation, they immediately moved Jay to ICU and the steady stream of specialists began coming to his room. Infectious disease doctors, neurologists, lung specialists, endocrinologists, and radiologists traveled through.

The parade continued, increasing in numbers. The pattern didn't change. The specialists never talked to Jay. They walked into his room and out of his room. The only time they acknowledge me is to badger me about the sin of prolonging Jay's death.

"What you must understand, "I explained to the neurologist, "is that you will feed Jay until his very last breath!"

"Well," he said, "we will just have to agree to disagree. You will just be prolonging the process."

"Sir," I said, "with all due respect, the doctors have been 'predicting' for approximately one year and four months now. Nothing they have said has been correct. I will agree to disagree with you, but you must hear what I have to say first . . . . I cannot prolong the process. I don't have the knowledge, the power, the majesty. When my Lord is ready to take Jay home, he will take him. Your food, my pleading, nothing, will stop it."

"There is something about dying with dignity," he answered.

"Really," I asked? "Then picture these two scenarios. You withhold nutrients from this man over here. He becomes pallid, emaciated, and begins to experience pain. You give him morphine and drug him out of his brain. However, you provide nutrients for this person over here. She is comfortable. She has rosy cheeks and is not in pain. You don't administer morphine. Now, sir, which died with dignity?

One day I entered Jay's room. He was especially lethargic. He was not responding in his usual manner and I noticed his tongue was swollen. I questioned the nurse. "Do any of the medications that you are giving Jay cause the tongue to swell?" I asked.

"No," she responded.

"Are you giving Jay his thyroid medication?"

"He is not on thyroid medication," she said.

"Yes, he is," I blurted. "He has taken a large dose of thyroid for over thirty years!"

She walked over to the computer. "No," she said, "Jay is not getting any thyroid medication."

"When did you take it away from him," I pressed. "He has to have his thyroid meds! He becomes lethargic, unresponsive, thick-tongued, and slow when he is low on this medication. You won't know if his symptoms are from the brain tumor or the lack of thyroid. He must have his thyroid medication!"

The problems were ongoing. There was no rest. I was getting emotionally, physically, and mentally fatigued. I called Rose, "When you come to the hospital, please bring a lawn lounge chair," I said. "There are only hard, straight chairs in the ICU waiting room. I am not leaving the hospital even though I can't be in the ICU at night. I'll just set up the lounge chair in the corner of the waiting room."

Rose brought me a chair and I set up quarters in an out-of-the-way place in the ICU waiting room. I stayed one night. Then the ICU waiting room volunteers came to me, "You can't sleep here," they said. "That is the reason the chairs don't recline. You'll have to go to a motel."

"Direct me to your hospital customer service representative," I said. "I mean the top person over the entire hospital."

When I met with the customer service representative, I said, "You may kick me out of the ICU waiting room if you like. However, you must understand that I will not leave the hospital with my husband, my best friend, in ICU. So when you kick me out of the waiting room, I will take my pillows and make a bed on the floor just outside the ICU doors. And if you remove me from there, the media will not be kind to you!"

The hospital gave me an empty room in the hospital without cost. It was in the maternity ward, one of the most secure rooms in the hospital. I spent the next two months there.

"We are in a hell hole," I told Rose. "In the mornings, I walk into Jay's room and it is dark. There is no music on the radio or the television. The curtains are pulled. There is no stimulus. Sometimes his nutrient bag is empty. They have buried Jay. What are we going to do?"

We complained to the doctors, we complained to the nurses, we complained to anyone who would listen. Finally, an oncologist who was tired of my tirades said, "We have a palliative care doctor. Would you like to visit with her and have her pull Jay's case together?"

My answer was a resounding "Yes!"

The family met with the palliative care team. They explained that palliative care is a new movement within health care. It is different from hospice because it is curative first and the patient is not 'locked' into a six-month life expectancy. Treatment is designed to follow the family's direction. Social workers, clergy, doctors, and nurses make up the palliative care team.

Rose summed up our feelings in the palliative care family meeting, "We are an upstream family in a downstream society. We love Jay and we want to care for him, honor him and his wishes, and support him with 'real' healthcare.

Society, especially American healthcare, is focused on death. They urge us to keep Jay down, in emotional pain, and without supports. They want to expedite his death."

Later, I asked Rose what made her think of the upstream family analogy. "I dreamed it," she said. "I dreamed that our family was swimming upstream and all these dead bodies were floating downstream, hitting us. We worked and worked to get upstream, but we were constantly moving around, pushing away, and working through the dead bodies!"

Rhonda visited with the palliative care team, requesting we establish official care directives. As a result, the family established guidelines for Jay's care through the palliative care team.

The results were:

Jay was not in pain. He never had experienced pain. So

morphine was taken off his treatment list. The only way the nurses could administer morphine was through a chain process. If the nurse on duty suspected Jay was in pain, she had to call me, Jay's wife. If I decided Jay was hurting, the nurses could call the palliative care doctor for orders.

When the nurses came to me, saying Jay was in pain. I would ask, "Did you ask Jay if he is in pain?" They would always answer, "No, but he is grimacing."

So I would visit Jay in the ICU and have the following conversation with him:

"Jay, sweetheart, are you hurting?"

"No," he would respond.

"Are you uncomfortable?" I continued.

"Yes," he would say.

I instructed the nurses to ask these two questions. Then I said, "Raise the blanket. If his left knee is straight, put a bend in it. Then reposition him in bed." (This is nursing 101! I'm not a nurse; I'm a communicator!)

A couple of the nurses actually stood in the hospital corridor and cried, saying I was abusing Jay. Palliative care called the skin specialist and she ordered an air mattress. The problem was solved. Jay didn't receive any more morphine and he never grimaced again. *Real comfort care* was the answer.

Care instructions mandated Jay would receive water and nutrition until his very last breath. Jay looked good. He had rosy cheeks and he was comfortable. When people came to visit, they remarked, "Jay doesn't look like he's fought cancer for over one year. He looks healthy enough to climb on his tractor and farm."

I always responded by saying, "That's because we aren't adding starvation to his other medical problems. We are providing nutritional support. We are giving him real comfort care!"

We began to look at life once again rather than death. We learned that very, very ill patients may be moved from one institution to another via Mercy Flights. The palliative care doctor called Duke University. They said if Jay could be weaned from the respirator, they had medication they were willing to give him. So that became our goal, weaning him off the respirator so he could travel to North Carolina.

We also learned that if a drug has passed through Phase II testing and shows promise for the patient's particular illness, the drug may be given for compassionate use. So Jay could have had experimental drugs from the time the Temodar lost its punch. He didn't need to qualify for a study. However, until we met the palliative care team, no one bothered to tell us this information.

Did we think we had won the battle? No, we knew we were in the fight of our life. However, we had finally found someone to speak for us, to support us, to view Jay as a living, breathing being - someone worthy of the resources he was using. If problems raised their ugly heads, we conferred with the palliative care team.

Good things had been put into motion. However, the bed of roses still had plenty of thorns. We were continually badgered by the specialists, by the clergy, and by some nurses to let go. Some of the language they used included: If you had the faith, you could let him go, fear will not help you, he will die anyway, you should consider what you are doing to him.

My night terrors continued . . . .

I screamed, "Oh, no, I am having a nightmare, but I can't wake up. I'm having a nightmare, but I can't stop!" The marbled face thief came after me with a long, long fork. The fork was so long it could reach me from a distance.

I tried to fill Jay's dinner plate, but as I put a piece of food on the plate, the marbled faced night-thief jabbed his fork into it, snatching it, stealing it, and escaping with it.

"Please, please," I begged. "I am filling my husband's dinner plate. Don't take the food. He needs this nutrition. He needs the food to keep him strong."

All night long, I begged. I worked, putting food on the plate. But the marbled-face thief kept taking it off.

When I awoke, I was gasping for breath. I had worked very hard all night long, but the plate was as empty as when I started. I cried.

Negligence - A Cancer Devouring Healthcare

It requires almost a stroke of luck to enter a US hospital and receive precisely the right treatment - no more, and no less. A landmark Rand Corp. study published in 2003 found that adults in the US received on average, just 54.9% of recommended care for their conditions. Average blood sugar was not measured regularly for 24% of diabetes patients. More than half of all people with hypertension did not have their blood pressure under control; one-third of asthma patients eligible to get inhaled steroids did not get them. (Gibbs and Bower, 2006)

Doctors

The oncologist responsible for Jay's care disappeared like the oncologist in our home city. After our heated conversation in the hospital corridor regarding Jay's request for food, we never saw him again. He didn't remove his name from the physician list on Jay's records. He remained listed as Jay's primary care physician. So the nurses were required to call him first in the event of a crisis.

The nurses in ICU reported that the oncologist wouldn't answer their calls or their questions. They said his response was, "I can't do anymore." So they called other specialists farther down on the list until they found someone who would respond to their questions. One nurse announced in front of everyone who could hear, "I'm not calling him again!"

One nurse told me that Jay was not putting out any urine. She called the doctor and he told her, "I can't do anymore." So she just let it go. However, when the night nurse arrived, he reported calling the doctor also. He received the same reply - 'can't do anymore.' However he refused to submit. Instead, he began to investigate.

Deciding the catheter may be clogged, he removed the catheter to check the line. Urine began pouring out all over the bed. After the spillage, the nurse still measured over 400 cc. The catheter was plugged. Jay was putting out urine, but it was being held in his bladder due to medical negligence. Once again, Jay suffered at the hands of incompetence.

Not one doctor came to Jay's rescue. The politics, the self-righteous attitudes, and their determination to have it "their way" prevented them from serving the patient!

The lung doctor was especially obnoxious. Standing right beside Jay's bed, he began to rant. "When young people go into a coma, they have a chance for recovery. When we old people go into a coma, we don't come out of them."

"Sir," I said looking up from my book, "either I don't know what a coma is or Jay is not in one."

"He's like this every time I come into the room." He snapped. "He never responds to me."

"Yes," I thought without saying anything," and you rush through somewhat like a jet. You never stop. You never try. You just scream at him. He will not respond to screaming. Never did. Never will."

Then I said, "Well, sir, he responds to me."

"Show me then," he demanded.

Jay was sleeping, but I stood up and walked around his bed. I placed my hands tenderly on his cheeks and said very softly, "Jay, sweetheart, I love you. I need to talk to you. Will you open your eyes for me, please?"

Immediately, Jay opened his precious, sweet eyes and looked at me with devoted love.

"The doctor is standing here," I said. "He wants to know what you understand. Will you shake your head yes for him?"

Jay shook his head yes. I thanked him and looked up at the doctor. "Did you see that?" I asked.

"Yes," he spit. Then he stomped out of the room.

This doctor is the same doctor that stood beside Jay's bed earlier and told me Jay had some congestion in his lungs. "I could put a vibrator on Jay's chest to loosen up the pockets of phlegm, but I really don't want to do that," he said, "because Jay is going to die anyway."

I was immediately angry. "Really," I asked. "Well, I'll tell you what. I'll agree with you doing nothing if you will march throughout this entire hospital and take life supports, medications, and other essential equipment off every person suffering from cirrhosis of the liver, emphysema, morbid obesity with multiple medical issues, AIDS, kidney failure, or any other virtual terminal illness." Demonstrating his total disdain for me, he stomped out of Jay's room without another word.

One day in the palliative care meeting, I said, "Doctor, you said that both you and the nurse will be out of town this weekend for personal reasons. We all know that the oncologist has dismissed himself from Jay's case and that no one from his oncology group has stepped in to fill the void. So you need to know, upfront, that if anything happens to Jay while you are out of town because the oncologist refuses to give orders, everyone will be in deep doo-doo!"

"I will be talking with the oncologist," the doctor said. "I'll get him back on board."

"Good luck," I warned. "He is arrogant and condescending!"

The next day, the palliative care doctor came into Jay's room to detail orders for the weekend. Then she said to the nurse, "I still have some issues to work through with the oncologist."

I immediately thought my prediction was correct. There was no way this little five-foot, petite doctor could match wits with a shrewd, calculating, vindictive male figure like the oncologist. However, to my surprise, the oncologist ordered two units of blood for Jay the next day. The palliative care doctor did make a difference this time.

Respiratory Therapist

The respiratory therapist was a petite woman with a sour face. She was not engaging like most of the respiratory therapists who provided Jay's care.

She was not anything like my favorite therapist, a middle-aged man who always talked to Jay, explained his every move to Jay, and watch him closely and expertly throughout the process of weaning him off the respirator. He was kind. He empathized with me and was wonderful.

When Sour Face came on duty and I knew Jay had drawn her for his care, I was greatly concerned. They were weaning Jay off the respirator. It was extremely important that he receive the utmost attention and care. She was evasive and rude. I did not trust her at all.

Mid-morning Jay began to make a gurgle sound. Jay's bed was not at the mandated thirty degrees for patients on respirators, so every time I came into his room, I raised the head of his bed. The therapist needed to clean his airways. I asked her to do that. She declined saying, "I clean airways at 2:00 this afternoon."

"He needs it now," I complained. "He is struggling to get air."

She refused. I asked her again and again. She continued to refuse. Just after lunch, Jay went into crisis. The therapist had to put him back on the respirator. I was livid!

I began talking loudly and distinctly to the palliative care doctor and nurse at the nurses' station. "There is no excuse for what happened to Jay today. I can't stand these insolent, hateful healthcare workers who should be on graveyard shift at the morgue instead of in this hospital."

"The therapist refused to care for my husband. She refused to keep his bed at thirty degrees. She refused to clean his airways. He suffered. He suffered because no one cared. He suffered because someone thought he should be dead!"

The doctor and nurse tried to calm me. I was crying and couldn't be calmed. They tried to smooth over the therapist's intentional insurrections.

"I'm not buying it," I said. "This is nursing 101! I want that therapist out of Jay's room. She is not to return for any reason! She is fired!"

The palliative care nurse walked over to Jay's records and wrote across them in red letters, "Keep the patient's bed raised to thirty degrees at all times." The respiratory nurse was banned from Jay's room.

The Nurses

The male nurses were wonderful - bar one. Is this a sexist statement? Not by me, but by the doctors standards according to the female nurses' reports. "The doctors are condescending and arrogant," the female nurses confided. "They talk down to us. They don't give female nurses the same credibility as they do the male nurses."

Male nurses, honest and secure in their positions, agreed they are treated differently by the doctors.

"Doctors, male or female, don't talk down to us," they said. "Most of us are going on to bigger and better things. Some of us want to be internists. Some of us are going to be anesthesiologists. Others want to be specialists. It's the politics of the trade. They don't want to burn bridges they may need later!"

This information explained why Jay had to endure an inflated, overly full bladder because the female nurse chose to do nothing. When the male nurse came on duty, he reacted to the same doctor, to the same rejection with action.

The female nurse knew the doctor in charge felt Jay was dying and that he couldn't help him any longer. Many female nurses in the four hospitals where Jay was a patient expressed fear in violating doctors' orders, thinking they might face dire consequences. They said reprimands would surely be a result of their actions and it could be as serious as retaliation or dismissal.

The male nurse had nothing to lose. Male nurses also talked freely. They reported feeling emotionally equal to the doctors. They knew in a few months, they would be viewing the doctors from another perspective.

They could perform their obligations and duties free from threat of reprimands or other consequences. Not one person male, female, nurse, or other hospital staff denied the powerful political agendas in medicine today.

Earlier, staff told me that Jay's slow heartbeat indicated the cancer had entered his vital organ system. I knew this was more of the same pressure to turn off the supports. "I know that's not true," I said. "I don't know where the cancer is, but I know a slow heart rate is not a sign of its progression."

"How do you know that?" they quizzed.

"Jay has always had a v-e-r-y slow heart rate." I said. "About fifteen years ago, his cardiologist put a monitor on him to make sure it was not too slow. He is a very laid-back person. When I asked the cardiologist about speeding Jay's heart up too much during exercise, he laughed at me.

He said. "'You can't get Jay's heart rate too high. It won't go there.'"

So the evening Jay's heart began to race, I was frightened. I talked to the nurse on duty about it. She pooh-poohed me, saying, "That rate is normal. I'll tell you what - when I start worrying - you can worry!"

"That will be a cold day in hell," I thought. "How dare you mock me?"

I went to visit with the head-floor nurse. He told me the nurse I visited with was one of his best nurses. "If I had sick family members, I would want her to be their nurse," he bragged. He is the one and only male nurse I held in contempt through Jay's entire fourteen-month experience.

I began to cry. "I know my husband," I said. "This is not normal and it is not okay. I'm just telling you this because you need to know." I left in tears to go up to my room for the night. I didn't sleep.

The next morning I learned that Jay was in crisis during the night. The quickened heart rate was the result of a new infection. The nurse called the infectious disease doctors in the night and they prescribed more antibiotics.

The Clergy

She walked into Jay's room. Our relationship during Jay's illness had been lukewarm at best. I had learned to be very guarded when clergy approached, and this one always gave me pause.

I was sitting in a chair at the foot of Jay's bed. She sat on a stool with wheels and rolled it over in front of me. She bent over and leaned toward me, "What will it take," she said.

"What will it take for what," I asked?

"What will it take for you to let Jay go. . . . His death?"

"Yes," I said curtly, "that might be a starter."

Then I put my magazine down on the table, stood up and walked out of the room.

She remained. She sat there on her preaching stool and watched me go.

Our pastor was my rock. He was an invaluable resource to me from a personal perspective, a medical perspective, and a spiritual perspective. His dedication, understanding, and support helped me tolerate the insincere, purchased clergy in the hospital setting.

One day, two angels with invisible wings came to Jay's room. They asked me what they could do for me. In jest, I answered, "I guess what I need at this very moment is a good old-fashioned minister, just like our own pastor to visit with me."

To my surprise, a very engaging, wonderful African-American minister came to Jay's room that evening and said he heard that I wanted to talk to him.

I was amazed, but jumped at the chance. I knew this man would have the same heart that I did. I knew I would identify with his soul and his words.

We went to a little conference room off the hospital library area. "I knew exactly what you wanted when I heard that you wanted to talk to me," he said.

"You wanted to hear a like-mind say that Jesus Christ is King and He will have the last word. If He chooses to heal, He will heal. If He chooses to take Jay home, He will take him home. Whatever His answer, you are willing to wait for the miracle – healing or calling. Praise God and to Him be the Glory!"

This meeting made the icicles drip. I loved this man through Christ instantly. He knew my heart because we were brother and sister in Christ. He heard me before I said it. It was refreshing. It was reassuring. It was healing.

On the Farm

In the Army

Retire from KDOT

Fun at Retirement

Jay at our wedding.

Wedding picture

Jay and I relaxing

Part 2:

It's All About the Money, Honey

Deaf Ear

The current system in America is the best possible way to transfer massive amounts of wealth from the American people to the drug industry and other medical industries. Our medical science has become deeply flawed, manipulated to serve corporate interests. (Abramson, 2005)

Medicine Out of Control, Fabrication, Chaotic System, Corporate Crime, Fraud, Conflict of Interests, Gouger's Paradise, Illegal Kickbacks – are words doctors, whistle blowers, consumer protection groups, and others use to describe the American Healthcare System.

Yet we Americans wonder how the Taliban could gain a stronghold in a country with intelligent people. We, a free people in a free nation, have allowed a monstrous healthcare system to hold us hostage for the past two decades. We won't listen when those, in the know, wave red flags, describe the abuse and gouging, and map ways to escape our chaotic condition.

America's healthcare tragedy began in 1973. Federal law made insurance companies magistrates over American healthcare, allowing them to both finance and deliver healthcare. The following documented truths from 1991 to 2005 depict years of warnings given to a deaf people.

February 24, 1991, a heading in the Daily Telegraph Mirror stated "*Medical 'Ignorance' is costing us billions.*"

Dr. Linda Peeno's 1996 Congressional testimony:
"*We have created a monster system, one in which among other transgressions, a physician can receive a high income for doing the*

reverse of the profession. Instead of delivering care, a physician can be significantly rewarded for denying it."

In his book, *Overdo$ed America, 2005*, John Abramson M. D. wrote: *"What I found over the next two years of 'researching the research' is a scandal in medical science that is at least the equivalent of any of the recent corporate scandals that have shaken Americans' confidence in the integrity of the corporate and financial worlds."*

Donald L. Bartlett and James B. Steele stated in their book *"Critical Condition"*, 2006: *"When you hear a politician, an economist, a corporate executive, talk about the wonders of the free market in health care, they neglect to mention the system is rigged in a way that would not be tolerated in the sale of any other consumer product.*

At least in the supermarket you have a choice of whether to pay the going price. When it comes to the cancer treatment you need to live or the emergency care your sick child requires in the middle of the night, you have no choice."

Multitudes agree that the American healthcare system is swaddled in corruption, even though ideas for practical solutions and workable remedies differ.

The Qua-Brutal Team Becomes Big Medicinal Business
To what extent can a business contract away the rights of another? To what degree can they contract to interfere with the needs of another? (Linda Peeno, Congressional Testimony, 1996)

The qua-brutal team - Big Insurance, Big Medicine, Big Pharma, and Big Government - have joined ranks to form Big Medicinal Business. Each entity intersects compliments, protects, and pardons fellow conglomerate members, pushing the American consumer further in the background.

Big Business corruption is no secret. Stories hit American airwaves every day.

Businesses cut corners, restrict customer services, and violate the environment - all for the sake of a dollar.

Cruise ships dump human wastes in our waterways. Corporate Executive Officers (CEOs) are indicted for stealing from the customer, telephone companies bump customers without their knowledge, and credit card companies collaborate to raise interest rates for one late payment!

Big Medicinal business is the same. They cut corners, restrict customer services, and sacrifice our safety. Hospitals hire fewer registered nurses and employ more nurse aides.

Too many hospital aides and other unskilled workers acquire positions with very short, band-aid type training. Laypersons with minimal or no medical knowledge can challenge too many hospital caretakers, winning the medical expertise contest.

'Back-rubbing' is common among the Big Medicinal Business partners, allowing them to put dollars first, corporate interests' second and patient care last. The following are examples of incestuous relationships that harm consumers.

- The Food and Drug Administration waives conflict of interest policy, allowing those with financial ties to Big Pharma to vote on drug safety.

- Many federal legislators, state government officials, and other government employees accept gifts, campaign money from Big Medicine, Big Pharma, and Big Insurance in exchange for promises of support.

- Big Insurance negotiates health care prices with Big Medicine, providing an avenue for legal financial kickbacks.

- Big Government acquiesces Big Pharma, mandating vaccines, outlawing Canadian drugs, and policing the generic drug market.

- Big Medicine accepts the role of 'gatekeeper' for Big Insurance, putting corporate and insurance dollars before patient care.

Big Government

Big Government does not understand the needs of the needy. The higher in government one ascends the deeper in poverty his humanity descends. (Silliman, 2007)

Americans live in the most wonderful country in the world. The common man has money, power, freedom, luxuries, and opportunity. One system lending this prosperity to the masses is free enterprise. Free enterprise allows people to design, initiate, and orchestrate ventures, buying and selling at will.

However, no system is without flaws and all have potential for down-sides. The down-side in free enterprise is when a system begins to grow without restraint, morphing into something alien. These systems are called monopolies.

Free enterprise and monopolies are contradictory ideologies. Free enterprise is *inclusive*, sharing royalties, innovations, and customer base. There are enough resources to go around. However, monopolies are *exclusive*, gobbling resources, strangling competition, and corrupting the system.

Four American conglomerates, Big Government, Big Medicine, Big Pharma, and Big Insurance, have merged into one huge monopoly, pushing all other competitors out.

The only competition is within itself and usually amounts to competing to cut corners here to make money there, competing to make more profit this year than last year, competing to streamline services and fatten net worth. Monopolies don't have to compete for customers. They own them through coercion.

Competition in American medicine is on the *wrong level*. Competition should not be on the executive level where cuts compete with services, innovation competes with savings, and medicine competes with salaries. Competition must be at the physician level!

The consumer must have the power to say: "If you give me the care, if you stay on the top of your trade, if you understand my needs, I will use you as my personal care physician. If you cannot serve me in this way, I will go to the physician down the road who is willing to put me first!"

Dr. Peeno testified that she "saw no difference between for-profit and non-profit organizations' violations against the people." This is because there are four entities in the Big Medicinal monopoly and one of those is Big Government.

This suggests that socialized medicine is *not* America's answer. However, the people, the citizens of this great nation, must become active and demand a redesign of the protocol, a redesign that breaks the monopolies and puts the people first.

Socialized medicine trumps state-of-the-art healthcare. Socialized medicine stalemates, stagnates and places medical power in the wrong hands.

Socialized medicine would be medicine of the government, by the government, and for the government. Here are some reasons why:

Most government workers are dedicated, people oriented, caring individuals. They work under a civil-service system that gives them a certain amount of job protection. They are free to do their jobs in the best way they know how without threat of political dismissal . . . *most of the time.*

However, once a state employee reaches the level of appointed position, everything can and often does change. In this new position, the employee is no longer protected by the civil service system. They can and will be gone quickly with a change of venue, a change of politics, or a change in executive favoritism. So to remain, they must constantly appease the power.

Too many times the employees' focus becomes promotion, money, politics, back-rubbing, power, and forfeiting of personal values. This change can happen automatically as they bow to the power that placed them in the coveted position.

The person's core beliefs may remain; however, with a multitude of new agendas pressing inward, the people oriented actions are too often pushed outward. This is the phenomenon that birthed the expression, *"Central office does not have a clue what is happening on the frontline!"*

Socialized medicine would never stabilize. Americans would never know if their coverage was available or not available, if it was the same as yesterday or drastically changed. The top level of government seldom enjoys on- times. They function most often at off- times.

The off-times of government are the times when government leaders change. Governors are elected every four years and presidents are elected every four years. Governors and presidents aren't always elected in the same four-year period.

Every time - - -*every time* - - - the power changes, almost everything else changes!

Every new governor, every new president, has massive changes in mind. The first priority of every newcomer in office is to create his or her own legacy. What will their legacy be - changed healthcare rules, fewer hospitals, more mandated shots, greater number of people served in fewer hours?

This all depends upon the peripheral powers that 'wine and dine' or otherwise influence the bureaucracy for favorable decisions, including minority groups, special interest groups, other politicians who helped prepare the path for this particular person.

One owed to this group or that group or this person or that person is a known fact among government insiders.

As a government employee, my position was one-man under the appointed personnel line. My immediate supervisor was civil service. My supervisor's supervisor was appointed to the position. The deputy secretary of the government agency was next, the secretary, and then the governor.

In the sixteen years I worked for the State of Kansas, I saw talented, wonderful people dismissed in the middle of special, promising projects just because the other political party was voted into office.

I saw projects that workers labored over for one-two-three-years scrapped and put in file 13 because the concept didn't match the new political scheme.

In addition to the changes in governorships and presidents, state and federal legislators and department heads are incoming and outgoing on a continual basis. These changes also cause a downward sweep of waste, chaos, and upheaval in government. New, different, or more of the same special interests and lobbying dynamics also affect government at this level, maybe at an even more prolific rate.

The changes in government aren't all bad. Our government's

change in faces is a part of the checks and balances. Options for directional change are what make us free. It is what thwarts the ruler, the dictator.

However, Americans have become lazy. We don't monitor situations well. American healthcare suffers partly because we have failed to stay abreast of who is paying whom. Most of us can't name the recipients of favor money provided by special interest groups.

We Americans have the privilege and the responsibility to follow our elected representatives' records. We should do so with gusto. Healthcare contributors don't distribute favor-money to a specific political party, it is a non-partisan phenomenon.

In checking the records, we see the two government officials at the federal level who received the most dollars from the healthcare related industries were Hilary Clinton, Democratic U.S. Senator and 2008 presidential hopeful, and Nancy Johnson, Republican member of the U.S. House of Representatives.

According to the Center for Responsive Politics, Nancy Johnson ranked number two for receiving the most dollars from healthcare in 2006, coming in at $1,231,563. Hilary Clinton grabbed the number three spot, reportedly receiving $1,201,843. Rick Santorum, a Republican Senator from Pennsylvania, was in the number one position and was voted out of office in 2006.

In addition to other pitfalls in socialized medicine, fraud can't automatically be dismissed. Anyone who listens to the daily news knows that fraud issues raise their ugly heads in government from time to time

In September, 2000, Dennis Cauchon wrote for *USA Today*, "FDA Advisors Tied to Industry."

"More than half of the experts hired to advise the government on the safety and effectiveness of medicine," the article said, "have financial relationships with the pharmaceutical companies that will be helped or hurt by their decisions, a *USA Today* study found."

In August 2005, *News Target.com* printed Manette Loudon's interview with Dr. David Graham, a Senior Drug and Safety Researcher at the FDA. Dr. Graham, speaking under protection of the Whistleblowers Act, made information about the drug Vioxx available to the public. This information documented Big Pharma and Big Government's joint effort to market a drug with known potential disastrous side effects to the people of this country.

Stephanie Saul wrote in the *New York Times* in September 2006, "Former FDA Chief Charged with Conflict of Interests."

The article said, "Dr. Crawford, who resigned abruptly in September 2005, just two months after his nomination had been approved by the Senate, is expected to plead guilty in federal court in Washington today."

Sudden changes can and do happen at the whim of government officials high enough in the ranks to make the decision.

Governors may: arbitrarily mandate vaccines, refuse to investigate abortion clinics, call in the National Guard, and make decisions that citizens feel are the publics' call.

These officials could also change America's healthcare in a moment's notice without our knowledge and without our permission!

In 2007, Texas Governor Rick Perry signed an order to mandate the Gardasil vaccine for all little girls entering the sixth grade. Reports indicate that Merck and Company, the pharmaceutical company that made the vaccine, lobbied furiously in Texas to accomplish this goal.

The Gardasil vaccine protects against four strains of human papilloma virus (HPV) that may cause cervical cancer. However, since cervical cancer rarely strikes children with underdeveloped reproductive systems and since the disease is sexually transmitted, many American families were shocked and outraged by Perry's decision.

He mandated the vaccine through an executive order that gave him the freedom to sidestep the Texas legislative bodies in the process. Therefore, one man with one idea and an alleged connection to Big Pharma changed the lives of hundreds of thousands of little girls and their families. It just took a stroke of the pen.

According to a CBS and Associated Press Internet report, Governor Perry allegedly has ties to Merck and Company.

The report states that Mike Toomey, a lobbyist for Merck and Company, was the governor's former chief of staff and alleges

Perry received money from the pharmaceutical company in his reelection campaign. *(MSNBC, Associated Press, Feb. 3, 2007)*

Secrecy surrounds the amount of money Merck and Company spent in its lobbying efforts in Texas. The spokesperson for the giant pharmaceutical company refused to elaborate.

After a public outcry, a group of Texas legislators requested that Perry rescind the executive order regarding the vaccine mandate, according to the *Houston Chronicle*. However, the governor refused the request!

This Texas mandate affects 365,000 young girls annually; however, it could as easily have been a mandate that affected the entire Texas population. That's the power one man may exert.

Since the Texas Legislature was not included in the Gardasil mandate and since Merck and Company allegedly poured money into the Gardasil lobbying efforts and into the governor's campaign, we might ask the question:

Did Merck and Company, without credentials and without the people's vote, make and enforce law in the Lone Star State?

Now that we have expounded on the activities of the Republican governor in the state of Texas, let us move on to another person, another political party -- Democratic Governor Kathleen Sebelius in the State of Kansas.

The following story was a hot topic throughout Kansas and brought national notoriety to the Wheat State.

In September 2003, Krishna Rajanna was an abortionist. One day he called the police to report a theft at his place of business, Medical and Surgical Services in Kansas City, Kansas. Detective William Howard of the Kansas City Police Department responded to the summons.

Howard said he was totally unprepared for what he saw at the abortion mill, the *Kansas City Star* and other local newspapers reported. The detective shared his chagrin with the public.

"I thought I had heard and seen every vile, disgusting crime scene, but I was in for a new shock when I started this investigation," he said.

At a testimony before the Kansas House Committee on Health and Human Services in March 2005, the detective alleged the following conditions inside the abortion mill.

There were grave sanitary violations. The abortionist was unkempt and filthy. He emitted a strong, foul body odor and the premises were filthy.

There were no visible hazardous waste containers, dirty dishes covered the sink and table, trash was littered throughout the domain, and roaches were crawling on the countertops. The room was dark, dingy and stinking.

Two dishwashers were positioned beside the toilet and were used as sanitizers for equipment, according to abortion clinic staff. The toilets were bloody and looked like human waste disposals. Blood was all over the floor. Biohazard trash, open drug containers, and a gas lawn mower blocked the back door. Styrofoam cups in the refrigerator stored parts of aborted fetuses along with food and drink.

According to some of the employees, Detective Howard reported, Rajanna allegedly stirred bits of the aborted fetuses in with his food and ate them.

The Kansas State Board of Healing Arts voted unanimously to revoke Rajanna's license, noting that in 2000 and 2001 they had disciplined Rajanna because "He didn't properly test his patient's blood and improperly labeled medications."

Subsequent to this trail of events, the Kansas legislature approved a bill that would require abortion clinics to obtain an annual license from the Department of Health and Environment.

In addition, the clinics would be required to hire surgeons as medical directors, report patient deaths to the state within a day, set standards for equipment, medical screenings, ventilation, and lighting.

Governor Sebelius vetoed this bill twice. Her argument was that medical professionals should set standards for abortion clinics, not legislators. Did her decision to veto these bills suggest that people aren't a primary consideration?

The issue wasn't an issue of pro-abortion or anti-abortion. The issue was safety for the women utilizing the services. Did Sebelius' pro-choice stance affect her decision in this case?

The question is not which side of the abortion argument America supports. The question is whether we understand that government officials have the power to change things at a moment's notice, perhaps making choices that reflect their personal ideology or political ambitions. Political discernment in medicine is a travesty. There should only be medicinal discernment in medicine.

In addition, Americans who push for socialized medicine also may be discounting or minimizing recent government history. The government has contracted out multiple services to for-profit groups in the recent past. These groups are called 'Contracted Providers.' This arrangement adds a for-profit middle-market to provide social services. Middle-men always increase product and service costs. They never decrease them!

In the late 80s, I underwent a delicate oral surgery procedure in Colorado Springs, Colorado. When I met with the doctor for my dismissal appointment, the doctor said, "I am retiring from medicine."

Shocked, I said, "You are a young doctor. You perform specialized surgery every day, correcting deformities and gross medical problems that change peoples' lives. Why would you quit the profession?"

"Our country is entering into socialized medicine," he said. "Socialized medicine does not honor physicians who strive to be the best, physicians who specialize within the specialty."

"Socialized medicine values the mediocre. It honors the followers, the emulators. I won't be a part of that system. That is not who I am!"

In addition, to misplaced power, instability, and outside agendas, *fatal attractions* are also a grave danger in socialized medicine. *Fatal attractions* are deadly for everyone.

Dr. John Abramson took a sabbatical from his medical profession to write his book *Overdo$ed America*. In this book, he exposed the fatal attraction between the FDA and Big Pharma.

The information in his book is timely, revealing, frightening, and combustible. It is personal to every American. It should burn us 'country folks' right out of our chairs, making us demand, "Justice now!"

However, in his book, Dr. Abramson also stated that he was amazed the information about Big Pharma's corruption raised so little emotion among the people. He expected an outrage, but only received a spark.

Are Americans not ready to make personal healthcare decisions? Do we really want our medicinal protocols and mandates dictated and changed through the whims of the elite? Do we want our healthcare decisions made by government officials who receive lucrative gifts from the very industry they are elected to regulate?

Abramson's lament of 'deaf ear' reminded me of the messages I heard in every government class, every social studies class, and in every history class throughout high school.

"When a people become apathetic, when a people become numb to their situation, when the people stop demanding what they deserve, the country is 'ripe' for takeover."

We must put the people back in the driver's seat, demanding Government accountability.

Sometimes it takes more than a voice. Sometimes it takes action. We know that hand-slapping doesn't work, and reprimands make no difference. Therefore, we must demand that government wipe the slate clean. Legislators must remove themselves from the "take." We need a *new* FDA.

Loyalties, favors, and objectives are colored by the money-bond. If legislators can't break free from this bondage, we must elect legislators who can. Once we have legislators autonomous and free, they will stop talking *about* the FDA! They will step forward and take action, initiating solid, permanent, lasting, customer friendly changes – today!

Big Insurance

Managed Care
The public has an essential role to play in insisting companies keep their priorities straight. (Weber, 2006)

Managed care is just that - removed third parties managing the patient's healthcare. This system has one main priority - low cost/high profit. Executives use graphs, pie charts, statistics, templates, and theory to scrutinize and regulate American's healthcare from afar. Patient history, family history, and other personal information are obsolete.

Everything is measured by dollars. Managed care pressures doctors to spend less and less time with the patient, mandating thirty-minute patient appointments be reduced to fifteen minutes regardless of the patient's concerns!

In many systems, the doctor or hospital negotiates a 'price tag' for a particular illness, disease, or hospital stay. 'Savings' from this negotiated amount is *free* money for the treating doctors and hospital. This is called gain-sharing. It is, in essence, a legal kickback!

The 'savings' are dependent upon patient outcomes. However, the accepted outcomes aren't good healthcare, patient satisfaction, or even appropriate treatment. The *only* outcome that matters is: Was the patient expediently removed from care. In plain street language, get rid of him and do it quickly!

Therefore, if a patient is terminal, expediting death will remove him from care. Sending a patient, who is recovering from illness, home early will remove him from care. The patient's removal from care, regardless of the means, allows doctors and hospital to share in the 'savings' from the original negotiated dollar amount.

If complications occur and patient care is prolonged, the doctor and hospital *lose* money on the deal. Therefore, it is imperative to move the patient, either by death or dismissal, as early as possible.

Money is the prize; successful treatment is not. Money is paramount; the patient is incidental. The patients' only purpose is to provide the money source through their personal dollars or insurance premiums.

Managed care is massive injustice for the patient. With the focus on cash, the patient as a person is nullified. A gentleman who lost his life in Arizona is a case-in-point:

Rob had asthma all his life. Even though he had asthma attacks from time to time as he was growing up, he was determined. He was known for focusing on his strengths rather than his weaknesses. In high school he played football and took part in other sport activities.

Later, as an adult, Rob worked for the local power company. For thirty years, he climbed electrical poles for a living. He was a pusher and a doer, so he received timely promotions and greater responsibility. Asthma was a reality in his life, but it was not the director of his life.

In 2002, Rob, in his early sixties, was admitted to a nationally known hospital to treat diverticulitis. Diverticulitis is little pit areas in the large intestine that have the potential to become infected.

After hospital staff mistakenly inserted a tube into Rob's lung rather than his stomach as intended, Rob became very ill. He later was diagnosed with a staph infection.

Rob and his family knew he was terribly ill. However, the doctor decided that Rob was ready to go home. Shocked that the doctor wanted to send him home, Rob begged the doctor for more time. "I'm too weak to go home," he begged. However, the doctor began the dismissal process without delay.

Rob's daughter intervened, explaining the family didn't feel Rob was ready to go home. She argued that he was still desperately ill. The doctor became belligerent and completed dismissal procedures.

The day after Rob returned home, he became violently ill. The family continued giving Rob his medications; however, the following morning, his family was sure they were losing him. He was struggling to maintain. They called 'Flight for Life', and flew Rob back to the hospital.

Rob died. Litigation ensued.

When the defense team realized the hospital would be held liable for Rob's death, they changed their defense strategy. They began to argue the *level* of medical negligence should be minimized, reducing retribution, because they said, "Rob would have died within three years anyway."

Surprised by the 'death anyway' argument, the prosecuting attorney questioned their reasoning. "How do you know that Rob would have died in three years?" he asked.

"Rob would have died within three years," they arrogantly projected, "because asthma would have killed him!"

The asthma defense argument worked. Even though the family did receive a settlement of an undisclosed amount, the court decreased the retribution amount. The fact that America's hospitals are notorious for being "killers from infectious diseases" was not a consideration.

Staph infection attacked Rob because he "was so sick," healthcare staff argued.

However, one wise nurse replied with an emphatic, "No!" She said that staph contamination must be present to contract staph infection. Eliminate the contamination and you will eliminate staph!

The family had no recourse. Big Medicine is securely connected to Big Government. According to Bartlett and Steele's Book *Critical Condition*, "Medical insurance pays, donating to Washington and lobbying with financial and emotional gusto, outspending energy, banks, and big tobacco in the lobby arena."

Managed care not only dictates patient care, doctor techniques, medical procedures, care price tags and service dumping, it also decides where to spend the consumers' insurance dollars.

Some insurance companies reportedly:

Pay for:	Deny:
Enhancing men's erections	Women's birth control
Abortions	Life-saving treatment for your baby
Organ transplant	Organ transplant rejection coverage

(Bartlett and Steele, 2006)

It doesn't have to make sense. It just has to make money.

We *must* understand managed care may do whatever it pleases. We, the consumers, don't have a voice. (*Remember?* We surrendered it.)

The Big Medicinal Business dupes Americans into thinking expensive healthcare is due to consumer law suits. We bow our heads in shameful apology. However, we must stop! We need to take inventory and compute a few numbers, proving that flagrant, unrestrained bureaucracies are to blame for the high healthcare costs.

As noted in the introduction, Big Pharma spends $15 to $18 billion a year in advertising costs. Healthcare executive salaries are reportedly well over $300,000 a year. In addition, according to Bartlett and Steele, "Nearly one of every three dollars spent on health care in this country goes for administrative costs. The United States spends a higher percentage of its healthcare dollars just to administer the system than any other country."

If these numbers aren't impressive enough, we can consider just one covered insurance cost to add to the list. It is a cost that many Americans voice an objection to paying - abortion.

America performs over 1,000,000 abortions each year. An estimated two-thirds of the American insurance companies cover all or partial costs for voluntary abortions. Abortions are advertised on the internet for $395 dollars. If insurance covers half the abortions performed each year, or 500,000, the initial cost is approximately $200 million a year.

These direct, up-front costs are only the beginning of the massive financial drain to the system and all consumers' pocketbooks. According to the Elliot Institute, ten percent of women who choose to have abortions suffer immediate complications from the procedure.

This means approximately 100,000 women a year will make claims to their insurance provider for abortion-related illnesses. Some of these immediate complications include: infection, excessive bleeding, perforation of the uterus, cervical injury and shock.

Long-term side effects from abortions present an even greater financial hardship on the system. Some of these complications include: pelvic inflammation disease, breast cancer, cervical, ovarian, and liver cancer.

Physicians for Life provides the following notations regarding the high risk of liver and cervical cancer following abortion on their website at www.physiciansforlife.org.

"A study of reproductive factors and the risk of primary liver cancer, conducted in Northern Italy between 1984-1991, found a 2.1 relative risk for liver cancer for two or more induced abortions and 1.6 relative risk factor for one abortion compared with women with no abortion history."

"A case- control study published in 1984 in France showed a 2.3 relative risk for cancer of the cervix for women with one abortion and a 4.92 relative risk for women reporting two or more induced abortions compared with women with no prior abortion history."

Services to cover abortion complications may include ambulance transport to a hospital, gynecological services, hospital stay, surgery, upgraded antibiotics, chemotherapy, and radiation. The financial toll on the American medical system has been estimated to reach over $1 billion.

In addition, to all abortion costs, the life of the mother may be in danger. According to Dr. David C. Reardon, Director of the Elliot Institute, abortion is four times deadlier than childbirth.

The Institute cites "the leading causes of maternal deaths within one week of surgery are hemorrhage, infection, embolism, anesthesia, and undiagnosed ectopic pregnancies."

One argument against the financial burden caused by abortion may be that live births are more expensive than abortions. If, in the number crunch, we discover the cost for the number of live births does outweigh the cost for abortions and ensuing complications, we might ask: Is cost savings the rationale for insurance covering abortions? Will terminating pregnancies actually boosts their profits? Providing abortion as a viable option to lower insurance expenditures does correspond to popular thinking today – if death is cheaper than life, let's cover death.

Americans Buy Illness

Iatrogenic illness must be included in the flagrant medical spending discussion. Iatrogenic illnesses are simply illnesses "brought on by a healer." Reasons for the onset of such illnesses include medical error, negligence, drug overdoses, and drug reactions. It is estimated that 44,000 to 98,000 unnecessary deaths occur in the United States each year due to medical errors.

The estimated annual cost to a 300 to 500 bed hospital in the United States due to medical errors is $1 million to $3 million, according to the *Wikipedia Encyclopedia*.

Medical errors may result from lack of communication, improper documentation, poor staffing, withholding drugs, or negligence. And nearly all of these causes can be attributed to decreasing time with the patients, cutting staff numbers, increasing patient loads, and increasing pressure on patients to leave the hospitals.

The list of iatrogenic illnesses Jay suffered is long. Most were the result of negligence and the need to hurry him out of the hospital due to Medicare rules. A short list to serve as examples of the causes and various iatrogenic illnesses Jay suffered include:

Cause	*Action*	*Result*
Negligence	Dylan tin overdose	Fall and injury
Negligence	Refused to suction	Returned to respirator
Negligence	Administered Ativan	Breathing distress
Negligence	Refused care	Sepsis
Negligence	Misplaced feeding tube	Staph infection

So far we have discussed $18 million for Big Pharma advertising, $200 million for surgery for individual "choice," and over $1 billion for treating complications resulting from that personal "choice."

We have talked about CEO and executive salaries reaching the $300,000 a year mark, and iatrogenic illnesses reaching $1 million to $3 million for each hospital with 100-500 bed capacity throughout the United States.

However, we have not even begun to talk about the following: other executive costs, U.S. efforts to inoculate world populations, executive waste, Viagra and other controversial drugs some believe are pushed for recreational use. We have barely begun the conversation about Big Medicinal Four's money extravaganza and we are already talking about billions of dollars, folks, not millions - *but billions*.

America is the richest nation in the world. We should be thinking of global health and extending our hand. So the issue is not whether we should support other nations. The issue is that CEOs and top-level government officials are spending billions of dollars at their own discretion, through their own mismanagement, without the payer's permission or knowledge.

As they continue to roll in the money, their finger remains pointed at you and me, the ones footing the bill, saying we go to court too often, we suffer from psychosomatic illnesses too often, we change doctors too often, and we sit around too often and get fat and get depressed, and get . . . and get . . .

Some politicians are saying we need socialized medicine because the people can't control their spending.

Rationing for Corporate Revenues

Remember, Dr. Linda Peeno testified, "We talk about rationing services, but never talk about rationing compensation for corporation." Watch Out, America! Managed care is the judge, the jury, the Gestapo for rationing decisions. According to Dr. Peeno, "a leading managed care textbook has fifty-two pages listed under *capitation*, but has only four pages dedicated to *ethics*. Every one of the references for *ethics* in this text discusses the concept as part of managed care's mission of rationing."

Dr. Peeno's 1996 testimony gives credence to the medical argument today because America's healthcare continues to decay. Many Americans are experiencing what Jay and I experienced in our fight for life. The system is using semantics to push us, to convince us, to overcome us. We hear about scarcity of resources.

According to Dr. Peeno, medical resources aren't scarce in this country.

The system gave and withheld drugs from Jay at will. They tried to pour medications into him that he didn't need. The narcotics, painkillers, desensitizers, and numbing concoctions were flowing until I stopped it.

However, they never offered life-support medication. G-CSF protein to boost his white cells or Erythropoietin to raise his red blood count or supplemental vitamins or blood transfusions was never mentioned to me as an ongoing support procedure.

That was quiet information that I didn't know about. It was not until *after* Jay's bout with sepsis that they gave him units of blood. These facts indicated to us that medication choices were not based on scarcity, but were based on money priorities.

They were managed care's version of rationing - rationing for dollars rather than care. If this example of medication rationing seems subtle the next example may be clearer:

Jay was receiving a food supplement at the hospital. It was essential that he receive a high fiber supplement because he had Decadron-induced diabetes. If the supplement was not high fiber, it would spike his blood sugar.

This spike in blood sugar would throw the insulin dose off balance and other complications ensued. Jay was gravely ill and every little adjustment was crucial to his comfort and well-being.

However, the hospital continually "ran out" of the high fiber food supplement, leaving the nurses no choice but to give Jay the sugar laden supplement.

The nurse explained that the hospital didn't want unneeded supplies stored on the shelves. It wasn't cost-effective. Since Jay's prognosis was death, it wouldn't be wise to keep it on the shelf and risk some left after he was gone.

They also didn't keep the sterilized bags of the supplement on hand so the nurse was compelled to open the can, dump it into a bag, and makeshift the process.

The danger was every time she handled the product, opening the can, fingering the bag, pouring the liquid into the bag, she took the chance of contaminating the product. Jay had a compromised immune system. He could not afford the chance.

Considering all the facts, I concluded there wasn't a shortage of the product. There wasn't a shortage of money. There wasn't a shortage of anything. The institution just wanted to make more money! Jay was incidental. Jay was secondary.

Dr. Peeno was correct. American healthcare does not refuse medications, procedures, life supports, surgery, or any other form of medical care because resources are limited. They refuse them because they may 'reduce' a very lucrative financial return, and that is the only reason!

"Americans receive the most expensive medical treatment in the world. However, in quality, it ranks thirtieth in the world," Dr. Abramson wrote.

To keep patients and families uninformed, pliable, and submissive to their agendas and to modern medicine's ideology, healthcare uses word games to take advantage of the layman's medical naiveté. They use words to soften, to imply, to subvert, to cajole.

Most of the time this tactic is successful, engaging in a full-court-press against the weak, the vulnerable, the frightened, the despairing. People in this condition want to trust. They need to trust because they may not know where else to go.

We have discussed semantics, strategies, the impact, the design in propaganda packages. However, Dr. Peeno gives this modern medical offensive strategy another name; she calls it *Ideological Indoctrination,* giving it the number one spot on her list of America's medicinal steps into total nothingness.

Before Jay and I were familiar with Dr. Peeno's testimony, we knew without a doubt that Ideological Indoctrination (which we called semantics) was the ploy medicine used to get us to submit.

The specific ways we experienced Ideological Indoctrination is through guilt tactics, money tactics, duty to sacrifice tactics, and the system is smarter, more experienced than you tactics.

Dr. Peeno suggested it includes the following rationalizations: "We are doing this in health care for the *good of society,* even if it requires some kind of sacrifice - even harm - at the level of the individual patient."

Number two on Dr. Peeno's list explains Jay's dilemma with the food supplement: *Emphasis on Efficiency.*

In Jay's case, it was a savings or increased-savings divide. It was unnecessary to keep the food supplement on the shelf because nurses could mix the concoction at bedside. The low fiber nutrient would raise the blood sugar, but the overall damage to the patient didn't warrant concern.

It is amazing that in 2007, I was complaining about every point Dr. Peeno had addressed in 1996, and I had never read anything about her. Her third step *Diffusion of Responsibility* was absolutely alive, detectable, and measurable with the doctors and hospitals Jay visited.

The buck never stopped. No one listened. It was never anyone's fault. I continued to express what we were facing, how medical care was responding, the damage incurred to Jay's body and his morale. Every time I mentioned it, every time I begged someone to listen, the response was, "I can only take care of now. I was not responsible for what happened earlier."

When the dancing-aid angered Jay by humiliating him and treating him like a two-year-old child, the head nurse blamed it on the patient. "He is suffering from Sundowner's," she said. When the hospital ran out of food supplement, the nurse blamed waste. When Jay fell in the hospital, they blamed it on the patient again. Even though Jay was drugged into delirium, they said, "The patient shouldn't have tried to get out of bed!"

Dr. Peeno's explanation of *Diffusion of Responsibility* is: "No one is responsible solely for adverse decisions."

Her fourth point is *Fragmentation of Behavior.* This actually may be the most frightening behavior of all! It is the most frightening because it is the first step, the essential step, for descending into the final three behaviors - *Disconnection of Conscience, Depersonalization of Beings,* and *Instrumentalist Thinking.* These last four behaviors describe prevalent actions during the German holocaust. They cement a Third Reich mentality.

Dr. Peeno's descriptions of the final four behaviors included the following:

Fragmentation of Behavior:
✓ "Acting one way in the role of work and different ways in other settings."

Disconnection of Conscience
✓ "Disconnecting conscience from conduct as a means to further insulate oneself from consequences."

Depersonalization of Beings:
✓ "Patients become statistic on a data sheet fractured into a lab result, an x-ray, a procedure, a profit "loss" or "saving," and approval or denial."

Instrumentalist Thinking:
✓ "Treating every action as a means to something else, rather than an end in itself."

Remember the doctor who wanted to withhold food from Jay? Let's revisit that scenario with Dr. Peeno's final four steps in mind.

The doctor motioned me into the hall. It was just he and I standing there - no witnesses, no contrary ideology, no colleagues, no clergy, no member of the palliative care team. He attacked me, telling me my husband was 78 years old, that he was dying, and he refused to hang a nutrient bag.

Then he walked into Jay's room and looked into his pleading eyes. He saw the tears and the emotion. He heard him say, "Yes, I want a feeding tube"; he heard him say, "I am hungry"; he heard the cries and the emotion from a man who was still very alive.

Jay was crying. Rose was crying. I was crying. The room was dripping in human emotion. In the midst of this, without a trickle of observable humanity, the doctor pivoted on the spot and spit the words out of his mouth like daggers stolen from street-crime, "I guess I'll have to do it then."

Would this doctor have acted the same way with colleagues, visitors, people with dissenting views, or the media at hand? Would he be a different man, at a different time, with a different audience, in a different place?

Was the doctor really there or was it just a human shell we saw? Did he see the emotion in my husband's eyes? Did he hear the pleading? Did he feel a tug at his heart? Did he see a man lying there or was his disconnect complete?

Was the doctor's mind in a distant mode that allowed him to bypass the emotion, the human connection, the possibilities, and probabilities? Did he see the money floating 'in' with Jay's death and floating 'out' with his care?

Was Jay no longer a man who could talk, and think, and feel? Or had he become a statistic instead? Was the end to the doctor's means the dollar, prestige, saving face, power, esteem?

If none of these, . . . what then? "

We have no ethical foundation if we are producing discord and destruction of human bodies and spirits." (Dr. Linda Peeno, 1996)

Big Medicine

It requires almost a stroke of luck to enter a US hospital and receive precisely the right treatment - no more, and no less. (Gibbs and Bower, 2006)

Big Medicine is really the most insignificant power among its colleagues in the Big Medicinal Business four. However, it is the power directly in touch with the patient, with the consumer, with each one of us. So Big Medicine actually yields the greatest, final punch in the process.

Big Medicine plays the role of "yes man" to the other three - Big Government, Big Insurance, and Big Pharma. They lay prone before them, providing services for the dollar.

This is why Jay and I were besieged with ongoing rhetoric to end the fight; this is why people die in American hospital emergency rooms, begging for someone to help them; this is why people mysteriously die in their hospital rooms and no one cares to investigate; this is why Rob was sent home too early and died upon his return to the hospital; this is why Terri Schiavo died at the hands of death mongers in an American healthcare institution while the country watched.

Big Government, Big Insurance, and Big Pharma have gagged, bound, and raped many doctors in this country. They have killed their ingenuity, their pride, their care, and their every day common sense. If I were the prosecuting attorney presenting the closing argument to the jury regarding the murder of America's physicians, I would say:

Members of the jury: Please feast your eyes upon these rich, arrogant, manipulating thieves - Big Government, Big Insurance, and Big Pharma. These thieves, who are suffering from a god-complex, have robbed America of any chance for state-of-the-art healthcare through their cold-blooded, calculated murder of the brilliance, the ingenuity, the drive, the expertise, the spontaneity and the care of the doctors in this nation.

They gagged our doctors, replacing truths with falsehoods. They bound our doctors, replacing action with inaction. They have raped our doctors beyond recognition, rendering them sterile and obsolete in the richest nation in the world, in the most powerful nation in the world, and in the most resource abundant nation in the world.

WE are the losers, dear jury. WE pay the price. If you think the problem has not touched you, your families, all of America, please don't look over your shoulder! If you do, you may be in for a grave surprise. These thieves have touched our pocketbooks, the caliber of our healthcare, our safety, and our personal healthcare choices! These maladies have touched us because our old-time family friend, our old-time confidante, our old time medical expert is dead!

So I am asking you -- consumer, jury, friend -- please give these three violent criminals what they deserve. Don't give them life in prison. They could escape someday. Don't give them a fine, a reprimand, a slap on the hand. They are murderers in the true sense. In the name of power, in the name of money, in the name of politics, they have silenced the medical innovators of this land, stripped freedom from the free, and clasped state-of-the-art health care in the bag. Give them the death penalty as they are – make them rebirth, regroup, reinvent, reform!

Replacing truths with falsehoods, replacing action with inaction, and raping our doctors beyond recognition, are documented every day with personal stories and other examples.

A few of these examples follow:

In Jay's case, the first and foremost documented evidence of falsehoods is: A doctor falsified hospital records. I have that record in hand. However, to prove this in court, we would have to call witnesses to the stand.

One witness would be the nurse of the attending physician who saw Jay without family approval. Would she tell the truth? The medical staff in Rob's litigation didn't. Even though their ploy didn't work, they still band together to save the institution.

Lies are a part of the process! Lies beget lies and the deceptive circus is ongoing. Picture this: The doctor who falsified hospital records lied. The doctor she summoned to Jay's bed side accused another doctor of lying as he stood there and lied. His statement: "Jay needs to be in a study. I just don't have one for him." was a blatant lie. This is why:

Jay did not have to qualify for a study at that stage of his illness. The stage of his illness alone qualified him for drug experimentation. It is called drugs for *"compassionate use."* A doctor later explained: A drug may be used for compassionate use if it has completed both Phase I and Phase II drug trials and shows promise for treating the disease and cancer from which the patient suffers. The drug does not have to pass through Phase III studies and it does not have to be FDA approved.

Later, Duke University School of Medicine said they did have a drug they would be willing to give Jay. However, this was after staff at the Kansas City hospital bungled the feeding tube placement and Jay had contracted a staph infection. He never sufficiently recovered from the infection to make the trip!

The doctor at Breech Medical Center should have visited with Duke University when Jay was there. The Center should have flown Jay directly to North Carolina on "mercy flight", by-passing the Kansas City hospital altogether.

This opportunity was missed through their negligence two months before Jay passed away. No one will know if the trip would have given Jay more time or if something learned in his treatment would have helped tens of thousands of people.

When the doctors first diagnosed Jay's condition, they told him that he would die in two months no matter what we did.

Ironically, Jay did not die until two months *after* the medical profession *refused* to give treatment for the cancer - *fourteen months later*!

Some people want to cut some slack for the doctors, saying, "Well, maybe they didn't know about Duke University or another aggressive treatment center."

My answer: I won't buy that. My general practitioner of yesterday had to know the best place to send patients for a multitude of illnesses. They had colleagues, medical friends all across the country and succeeded in sending us to where we needed to go. Many medical specialist offices today employ research personnel. If they don't have them, they may contact the hospital librarians who will get any information they request. Oncology is their business. It is their only business. They not only should know where to send the patient. The *must* know!

However, the point is to 'dump' the patient for financial

reasons. It is like playing 'hot potato.' They want the very sick out of their institutions fast. If they remain, it will cost them. Patient care is not the goal, money is!

Medical lies were rampant every day during Jay's illness.

Their negative predictions for Jay were cover up lies for inaction. If only one or two predictions had been wrong, or even a few, we might believe they were mistakes. However, *none* of them were true - not one. So is it safe to assume a plan ensued? Some of their predictions included:

- ***Jay will be dead in two months no matter what you do.***

Jay lived a good fourteen months, pain free and virtually seizure free.

- ***When the tumor is located in this area, patients pull away from family and friends.***

Jay always had me in mind. He worried about me. He joined in the grandchildren's fun, watching videos, laughing, and entering into their childhood scraps. Jay always suggested playing pool at the motels rather than just stay in the room. Nurses talked about how Jay looked at me with love until the day he quit opening his eyes! He never pulled away. Ever!

- ***Jay will be dead by the end of the week. Jay will be like a patient with Alzheimer disease. He will be unable to think through situations. Temodar won't produce immediate results. He must have IV fluids. You can't take care of him alone.***

Jay was not dead at the end of the week. Jay didn't need IV fluids. Temodar did result in immediate improvement. I did take care of him alone, exceeding home health and hospital care. Jay was not like a patient with Alzheimer disease because:

- ***Jay always knew what he didn't know.***

He knew he no longer could mentally maneuver roadmaps and road ways. He knew that is why he couldn't help me drive to Texas. He reasoned that he could no longer walk alone, so he asked for assistance. He knew his losses! Always!

- ***Jay always reasoned.***

When we bought the wheelchair accessible van, Jay's man-sense told him we needed to sell a vehicle, he said, "We need to sell the pickup then." He always responded appropriately when questioned or instructed to help in some way.

- ***Jay always knew family and friends.***

Jay always demonstrated through conversation gestures or tears that he recognized and loved the family.

If we must compare Jay's condition *with* something, I would say he became inquisitive, wide-eyed, and innocent like a child.

The family who loved him, helped him, and nurtured him throughout his illness gives a thumbs-up to this analysis.

The happy part of this is the goodness that came from Jay's spirit through this time. Jay's childlike nature was palatable for the family because this is how we knew him anyway. It was just more of the same.

We enjoyed him, we laughed at some of his antics, we cherished his open, loving responses. When I was employed by a Western Kansas school district, I worked with children with learning disabilities and children who were academically challenged. All of us working with these children knew one basic fact: Every child is gifted in some way and these children, regardless of their disabilities, were delights.

Jay was a delight, and the wonderful part of it was that when the Temodar was working, we saw instant, automatic improvement. He didn't have to relearn what he didn't know.

He automatically knew it again.

Many doctors throughout the country will contest these words. It doesn't matter. We saw it. We lived it. We know it. Some brain specialists throughout the country have said in essence, "Many doctors don't understand the brain's amazing ability to heal and regenerate itself."

We could continue to discuss the doctors' threats and doomsday rhetoric. However, these examples document the bended truth and outright lies that Jay was forced to endure.

So let's turn our attention to action turned into inaction and raping our doctors beyond recognition:

On May 9, 2007, Edith Isabel Rodriquez died in an American hospital emergency room because no one would come to her aid. Reports say that Rodriquez was bleeding from the mouth, she was writhing in pain, and her friend was pleading for help!

After his calls for help were ignored, he began to plead for 911 rescuers to come transfer the patient to another hospital.

They refused.

Rodriquez died in the middle of a hospital emergency room in the United States of America with a perforated bowel!

Rodriquez' chance for survival was excellent if she had been treated.

However, according to the Associated Press, the Los Angeles County Coroner's Office ruled Rodriquez' death accidental!

What is it that we don't get about this scenario? Doctors, nurses, medical staff are walking around this woman, ignoring her, refusing her, and we don't stand up and ring the phones off the hooks on our U.S. Senators and Congressmen's desks.

We excuse the behavior because it was a hospital in distress in California? No, it is a system in distress throughout America. It is happening all over the country. What happened to Rodriquez can happen to any of us.

I received a first-hand report from a woman in Nashville, Tennessee. She said:

"My father lives in Nashville, Tennessee, but the same thing happened to him as the woman in California. He had a heart attack and lay in the emergency room for seven hours before they took him back for treatment.

I was crying and said I would personally take him anywhere, somewhere. Hospital staff ignored me. They kept walking past my father, but would not help him. He almost died. Why do they get by with this? Why are people not yelling to the mountain tops?"

Have we closed our eyes? Have we closed our doors? Have we buried our brains? Do we realize that every violation, every misdeed, every study gone awry, and every untimely death is just waiting to knock on our own doors? We must stand up. We must become strong in the broken places. We must unite our voices, and say, "No!" . . . . . . But wait. There's more . . . .

Too many doctors and hospitals throughout America have become petty white-coat thieves. Medicare and Medicaid Fraud runs rampant.

When I worked for the State of Kansas, concerned consumers called and reported violations. "They charged $75 for an aspirin" or "Medicaid was charged for something that I didn't receive" or "The charge was not correct, it should only have been . . . . ."

People complained that when they reported fraud, it went nowhere. They said, "The people we report the fraud to just reply, '"That's just the way the system works. They always charge the state more. That's the name of the game. Don't worry - you didn't pay for it.'"

Many healthcare staff defends Medicaid fraud. They say, "There is no money in treating indigents in this country." Patient profiles make no difference. The patient age makes no difference. Money makes the difference. Medicaid fraud is prejudice against the poor. The following true story depicts just how bad it can get:

Rose and her husband took foster children into their home for a short time. Two of the children were precious African American boys, Tim and Tom. They were three-year-old twins. One day, Tim became very ill. Rose took him to the doctor. The doctor gave him medication and sent him home.

However, instead of getting better, Tim became worse. After he had a convulsion, the doctor finally admitted him to a Wichita, Kansas, hospital. They diagnosed Tim with pneumonia and kept him in the hospital for a couple of days. When the doctor dismissed Tim from the hospital, Rose was deeply concerned.

This was not Rose's first experience with a toddler with pneumonia. The other child was a little girl who was not on Medicaid. Her father was a teacher and she was covered by his policy. The doctors explained to Rose that a child recuperating from pneumonia should stay in the hospital for twenty-four hours after the fever breaks. They kept the child an extra day.

Tim's treatment was very different from the other child's experience. His fever had barely subsided. He was still lethargic. He didn't seem well.

Rose discussed this with the doctor, but he insisted the child was ready to go home.

On the way home, Tim vomited numerous times in the car. He was visibly very sick. When Rose returned to her home town approximately twenty minutes from Wichita, she went directly to her local doctor's office.

Angry, Rose confronted her doctor, "Why won't someone take care of this baby?" she asked. "Is it because he is on Medicaid or is it because he is black?"

The doctor jumped to attention. "We will take care of him," he said. "We will put him in the hospital until he is well."

The doctor put Tim back into the hospital and he was not released until he was well. Rose often wondered what would have happened to Tim if someone had not been there to advocate for him.

Some doctors prostitute themselves to Big Pharma. After being gagged, bound, and raped by the Big Medicinal Three, they had some choices to make.

They could leave medicine like the oral surgeon in Colorado Springs, Colorado; they could wing it alone or join a like-minded group and hope for survival; or they could become pawns in the scheme and be called *little brother.*

Some of those who joined the ranks to become the fourth member in the Big Medicinal Four became educators, consultants, and speakers for Big Pharma for big bucks.

Moving the patient down the priority list, they placed Big Pharma in the number one spot.

Those who are really dedicated to the cause may even play hard ball in selling pharmaceuticals to their patients. The following story is an example:

Sherry took her four girls, ages 15, 12, 10, and 4, to her doctor for school physicals. This doctor has a Pfizer Drug Educator plaque hanging on his wall. Drug representatives routinely hold up his patient appointment times fifteen to thirty minutes.

When Sherry entered the doctor's office, he asked, "Are you going to give your girls the Gardasil vaccine today?"

"No," Sherry answered. "We don't know enough about it yet."

"What are you going to do when the state mandates the shot?" he queried.

"I'll decline, giving my Catholic faith as a reason," Sherry said.

"You can't do that," he slammed. "If you were Mennonite and refused all shots, you might be able to give your faith as a reason. But Catholic won't do it."

"Won't you be sorry if your girls get cervical cancer," he continued to chide.

"No," Sherry said sticking to her convictions. "I will inform them they aren't protected. I will tell them if they choose the behavior, they also will choose the consequences."

"There is something called 'child abuse' when parents refuse to protect their children against invaders," the doctor threatened.

"I believe giving my child an inoculation with ingredients that aren't proven safe is a form of child abuse," Sherry countered.

"Well," the doctor retorted with disgust, "I have told my patients in the past to get another doctor if they don't want to do what I suggest."

Sherry left the doctor's office with a commitment to find another doctor!

The Last Straw

The last straw, the mark of distrust, is when doctors fear being treated by doctors.

In May 2006, *Time Magazine* printed an article "*What Doctors Hate About Hospitals,*" written by Nancy Gibbs and Amanda Bower. Some of the entries follow:

A pediatrician, Dr. Donald Berwick, said when his wife was in the hospital, "No day passed - not one - without a medication error. Tests were repeated, data misread, information lost. The errors were not rare; they were the norm."

Dr. Robert Johnson lost his career as a surgeon when a doctor bogged his wrist surgery.

Dr. Albert Wu, an internist, said, "Having a 'sitter' (for loved ones in the hospital) is something I advise people to do - and if they happen to be a professor of medicine, it's not a bad thing."

Doctors also complain on the local level, demonstrating once again the universality of America's healthcare dilemma.

A local doctor said he had a loved one who was dying from cancer. He tried in vain to suggest comfort care procedures to assist the patient through the ordeal. However, he said being a doctor himself didn't help. Their plan was outlined. Their strategy was decided. They simply wouldn't listen to him.

The story is summed up . . . The American healthcare system does not care who you are, how rich you are, how famous you are, how sick you are, or how desperate you are. It's all about the money, honey.

Big Pharma

The American public can no longer blindly trust that its valued medical journals and world-class medical experts put the interests of patients first. Becoming well informed and reclaiming personal responsibility are the best antidotes to a fundamentally flawed system. (Abramson, 2005)

One perfect example of the Stockholm Syndrome is American's relationship with big Pharma! Big Pharma financially gouges us, lies to us, makes laws against us, and kills us, and we continue to listen to them, accept them, forgive them and even brag about them.

The bookshelves are full of documented information regarding their violations against us, including: *Profits Before People* by Leonard J. Weber, *Truth About Drug Companies*, by Marcia Angell, M.D., *The Big Fix* by Katherine Greider, and *Overdo$ed America* by John Abramson, M.D.

Big Pharma has arranged many tidy little lies that keep them in power and in the bucks. Historically, academia and government spearheaded medical research. However, today Big Pharma spearheads pharmaceutical research from which they reap the benefits. They are financially tied to the outcomes. Conflict of interest goes unabated. Secrecy is a powerful tool in this ploy.

According to Abramson, "*Drug companies often keep the results of their studies secret, even from their own researchers, on the grounds that such results are 'proprietary information' of economic value.*" The only way this information may be accessed is through the Open Records Act.

This secrecy clause permits drug companies to issue only complimentary information regarding their drugs, resulting in many tragedies including the following Vioxx disaster:

According to Dr. Abramson, Merk and Company and FDA knew that Vioxx was a dangerous drug back in the year 2000.

They also knew that the drug wasn't any more effective than other pain relievers on the market.

However, they forged ahead, developing propaganda and marketing strategies. With Merck and Company and the FDA stoking physician sales efforts, doctors prescribed $7 billion worth of Vioxx. The rest of the story is history as tens of thousands of Americans suffered heart attacks and/or death.

The truth: Aleve was safer, cheaper and just as effective. (Abramson, 2005)

Later, the FDA organized a panel to advise on marketing Vioxx, Celebrex, and Bextra. After discussion and evaluation, the panel chose to endorse the continued marketing of these drugs.

The Center for Science in the Public Interest conducted background checks on the panel members. The results of those checks revealed that 10 of the 32 advisory consultants had direct financial ties with the drug companies. Some were consultants or speakers. Others had received research money from Big Pharma.

The Center for Science in the Public Interest concluded that if the ten advisors with conflict of interests had not cast their votes, the committee would have voted 14 to 8 to remove Vioxx from the market and 12 to 8 to remove Bextra. *(Weber, 2006)*

Even though government must follow policy and policy prohibits conflict of interests, there is also a secret on the government's side.

It is called a *waiver*. Government uses waivers all the time to excuse themselves from the rules - this time. The waiver must be approved by policymakers. However, any crafty writer can make a case for excusing the government agency from the rules in this particular situation.

They do it all the time. People have no guarantee that policy will reign, keeping the perpetrators at bay and the community safe.

British drug authorities warned their people that antidepressants increased suicidal thinking and behavior in children and adolescents. This information was based on nine studies that were also available to the FDA.

Subsequent to the British warning, the FDA convened an advisory committee to discuss the potential hazards that antidepressants posed for children and adolescents. The FDA had assigned one of their own epidemiologists to head up the investigation regarding the concern. However, when the committee convened, FDA removed the epidemiologist from the agenda, preventing him from giving a report. *(Abramson, 2005)*

Eighteen months after the British announcement and eight months after the FDA advisory committee met to discuss the drugs hazardous potential, the FDA belatedly mandated a warning on the drug label and a patient information sheet to outline the potential dangers.

Even though the drug companies own studies showed that antidepressants increased suicidal behavior in young people, they continued 'pushing' the drug regardless of the peril to our children. *(Abramson, 2005)*

They could do this, according to the *"proprietary information of economic value"* clause.

When people think of medical violations, they usually think of the elderly or even the disabled. However, what America does not understand in our brokenness is that when we disrespect and devalue one life, we disrespect and devalue all life.

The latest Big Pharma attempted financial sweep is their Gardasil scam!

Hundreds, thousands, maybe tens of thousands of parents are giving their little girls Gardasil, thinking they are protecting their daughters against a potential invader. However, too few have actually studied Gardasil information and asked the important questions.

After Texas mandated Gardasil for the children of their state, some Americans stepped forward. Their timely protests temporarily deterred Big Pharma's plan to continue the mandate-press in other targeted states.

Even though there are numerous value-based reasons why many people feel the Gardasil ploy is especially unethical, we will talk about purpose, safety, future ramifications, alternatives, and cost. After evaluating all the information, considering Big Pharma's deceptive history and measuring our trust of the system, we can make informed decisions.

Gardasil was designed to protect women from sexually transmitted HPV viruses that cause cervical cancer. There are 40 types of HPV viruses. Gardasil protects against four of them.

If Merk and Company is successful in mandating the vaccine throughout the nation, they rake in an estimated $3 billion dollars for the life of the patent.

Since Gardasil protects against only four of the cervical cancer types, Merck and Company are free to design another shot next year covering one - two - or five more types, calling it a "new drug," increasing its price, and placing it under a new patent for an extended windfall. This procedure may be repeated again, and again.

Was this in the original plan? Did Big Pharma intentionally design the vaccine to cover only four strains? Did they want to make a "me too" drug next year? Since Merck doesn't have to release all study information due to *proprietary information of economic value*, we may not have answers to these questions for several years.

Cervical cancer is not a lightning bolt! It does not enter the body and instantly ravage women's organs. The pathogens causing cervical cancer may take several years to manifest themselves into the disease.

Women in underdeveloped countries are at greater risk than women in the United States. Approximately 3,700 women die from cervical cancer in this country each year. Most of these women didn't have routine Pap smear tests.

Smear tests made available among America's poor and educating others to the value of the yearly test could virtually eliminate the dangers from this disease. Children with underdeveloped reproductive systems very seldom contract cervical cancer. Women over forty who are sexually active and woman who have had voluntary abortions are prime candidates for the disease.

Let's do the math. Merck and Company proposes inoculating multi-millions of teeny-bobbers at $360 each to prevent 3,700 deaths in adult women when regular smear tests would virtually eradicate the disease.

Remember, it doesn't have to make sense; it just has to make money.

Looking at the Gardasil vaccine through a mother's eyes, questions of safety are raised. The vaccine ingredients include four proteins. They are listed in the PDR as HPV 6 L1 protein, HPV

11 L1 protein, HPV 16 L1 protein, and HPV 18 L1 protein.

The origin of the proteins listed in the Gardasil ingredients is difficult for the average layperson to ascertain. However, the list raises many questions.

Historically, cattle, dog, rabbit, mice, and assorted insects have played a role in the development of vaccines. The PDR also indicates in some instances that cattle from other countries provided the protein substrates for other drugs dispensed in America.

The PDR also lists aborted fetal lung tissue (MRC-5 aborted embryo fibroblasts) as an ingredient in Merck and Company's Rubella and Hepatitis A vaccines.

Some sources do indicate that Gardasil contains DNA and bovine substrates. So are any of the proteins listed in the Gardasil vaccine from foreign cattle or aborted babies?

Other Gardasil ingredients include:

Amophous ***Aluminum*** (as hydroxyl phosphate sulfate ajuvant) is another Gardasil ingredient. Controversy is still brewing about whether mercury in vaccines has contributed to increased incidences of autism among America's children. Some reports indicate that aluminum is even more dangerous than mercury.

L-histidine is also listed as one of Gardasil ingredients. According to many reports, L-histidine should not be administered to pregnant women, nursing mothers, or children. The PDR echoes the warning that Gardasil should not be given to nursing or pregnant women. However, it recommends the vaccine for children as young as ten years old.

Sodium Borate is another ingredient in the Gardasil vaccine. Sodium Borate is contained in boric acid, a cockroach poison. Sodium borate poisoning may cause immediate or long lasting reactions. Historically, doctors used sodium borate to disinfect and treat wounds. According to the *New York Times* online, patients who received repeated boric acid wound treatment became "sick and some died." Because boric acid is now known to be a dangerous poison, it is no longer commonly used in medical preparations." (New York Times, Wednesday, Oct. 24, 2007)

HPV is a virus that only infects humans; however, animal studies were conducted to test Gardasil safety. It was administered to female rats to test for effects on mating performance, fertility, or embryonic/fetal survival.

Many scientists consider testing human medications on animals fraudulent. According to these professionals, animal testing, vivisection, will not produce reliable information for human implications. "Animals can't communicate psychological disturbances including headache, amnesia, nausea, or depression."

In addition, human reactions to medication and animal reactions to medication often present dichotomies.

Doctor Robert Sharpe provides the following examples:

- *Cortisone produces birth defects in mice but not people, but thalidomide works the other way around*

- *Morphine calms people but excites cats, goats and horses;*

- *Penicillin is highly poisonous to guinea pigs and hamsters;*

- *Insulin causes birth defects in animals but not in people;*

- *The antibiotic chloramphenicol produces the blood disease aplastic anemia in some human patients but it saves animals;*

- *In dogs, the muscle-relaxing drug tubocurarine causes a severe fall in blood pressure but is comparatively safe for people,*

- *Aspirin used in human therapeutics are poisonous to cats.*

The similarity between the rat's reproductive system and children's underdeveloped reproductive systems is difficult to comprehend. However, it *is* a test! If trouble brews in the future, Merck and Company can say, "We tested this on rats and it didn't pose a problem."

Merck and Company tested the rats for mating performance, fertility, and embryonic survival. Transposed this could read: We want to know if the vaccine will hinder my daughter's sexuality, her ability to have children, or my grandchildren's survival.

Anyone contemplating giving the Gardasil vaccine to their children might want to survey the PDR and examine reported birth anomalies in women who received the Gardasil vaccine during pregnancy.

According to the PDR, Merck and Company didn't test the Gardasil vaccine for cancer or gene damaging side-effects.

Hard Questions we <u>must</u> ask about Gardasil:

➤ What is the origin of the protein substrates in Gardasil? Are they plant proteins, animal proteins, insect proteins, or aborted human proteins?

➤ Why were these specific proteins selected for use? If they are bovine proteins, were the bovine from America or from a country plagued with mad cow disease?

➤ If any of the proteins in Gardasil are human aborted fetus proteins or animal proteins carrying misshaped prions, will my child develop Creutzfeldt-Jakob disease?

Prions are misshaped proteins that cause Creutzfeldt-Jakob disease. This is the human form of Bovine Spongiform Encephalopathy (BSE) or Mad Cow Disease.

Some scientists believe that Prions are encoded by the host individual or animal. Currently, there is no way to detect misshaped prions until after death from the disease.

➤ Why did Merck and Company test rats for subsequent reproductive and sterility complications? Did they test the rats for these specific complications because they pose the greatest threat to my child?

> ➢ Since puberty in humans is unique and my child's reproductive system is underdeveloped, what does a rat's mature reproductive system have to do my child's potential for post– vaccination complications?

> ➢ What human-animal dichotomies did you consider when choosing rats for testing?

> ➢ Why did you include aluminum in the ingredient list? How does it differ from mercury?

> ➢ Why is aluminum safer for my child as opposed to other metals?

> ➢ Why is L'histidine not recommended for children by many medical experts?

> ➢ Why did Merck and Company disregard the L'histidine warning?

> ➢ Why does Gardasil contain an ingredient, sodium borate that companies use to make rat, ant, and cockroach poison?

> ➢ Has Merck and Company initiated steps to investigate the reported deaths following Gardasil inoculations?

> ➢ Did Merck and Company withhold pertinent information regarding potential dangers to my child under the *proprietary information of 'economic value'* corporate protection clause?

> ➢ Is Merck and Company willing to publish **all** study information regarding the Gardasil vaccine, allowing independent doctors to issue an evaluation?

Prion Diseases

In the questions directed to Big Pharma regarding Gardasil, we mentioned two "brain-eating" diseases, Bovine Spongiform Encephalopathy (BSE) and Creutzfeldt-Jakob Disease (CJD). The prion, a term coined by Dr. Stanley Prusiner, was a common denominator in both these diseases.

The word prion is an acronym for PROteinaceous Infectious Particle. Dr. Prusiner won the Nobel Prize in Medicine in 1997 for his work identifying and mapping the characteristics of the prion protein.

The first thing about the prion that we must understand is that *we don't understand it.*

The prion and its relationship to 'brain-eating' diseases, is controversial and in the discovery stages at best. Doctors, scientists, and Big Pharma are still investigating and are still learning as the information continues to evolve. Theories abound.

However, in the laymen's eyes, the unknown information is pertinent and essential, helping us to protect ourselves and demand 'people before profits' from the Big Medicinal four. We must demand scientific caution in view of their uncertainty.

There are two discoveries that we must understand before we discuss the prions devastating potential for our generation. The following information was gleaned from the *Learn.Genetics, Genetic Science Learning Center* at the University of Utah.

Prions are strands of protein that characteristically fold themselves. If they begin to fold incorrectly they become antagonistic to the healthy prions and become violators of the host animal or human systems.

This happens because prions have the unique ability to reproduce themselves and they retain this ability in their misshapen form. So the misshapen prions begin to devour the normal proteins around them. As normal proteins are eliminated, the victim's brains become sponge-like, filled with holes and empty spots throughout.

This is the BSE or Mad Cow Disease in cows, and it is CJD or Kuru in humans, and it is called Scrapes in sheep.

Additional history on prion diseases follows:

The Fore (FOR- ya) Tribe of women and children of New Guinea cooked and ate their dead relatives. They considered it an honor to their loved ones and thought eating some of their ancestor's remains would make them smarter, more beautiful, and better human beings.

The custom in this New Guinea tribe was that the men and women lived apart. So the men very seldom or ever shared in the ritualistic eating of the familial parts at funeral gatherings.

During this time in the tribe's history, the women and children suffered from a strange and always fatal disease. The tribe named this disease Kuru.

Kuru means "trembling in fear." The first sign of the disease is staggering, scissor-gates, falling, and finally the inability to walk. The person stops chewing and can no longer swallow. With the inability to eat, the person begins to lose weight, becomes emaciated, and dies.

In the 1950's, a virologist who studied infectious diseases, Carleton Gajdusek, began to research the Kuru disease. After sending brain tissue to the United States for further study, Gajdusek concluded that Kuru had the same characteristics as CJD. It appeared to be an infectious disease that produced a sponge-like condition of the brain and depleted the immune system. *(University of Utah)*

In the 1980's and 90's there was an outbreak of mad cow disease, BSE, in Europe. According to some reports, over 150,000 livestock in Europe were infected with the disease and died. Then the disease transferred to humans and more than 100 people also died.

Prior to this outbreak scientists did not believe BSE or Scrape was transferrable to humans. So the question became: Why were cattle and humans in the same geographical area becoming afflicted with similar brain diseases? An intense investigation followed:

To increase protein in cattle feed, to accelerate bovine growth and the fattening process, British farmers began to feed their cattle ground meat, bone-meal and by-products from sheep.

In man's attempt to make an herbivore a carnivore, cows ingested misshaped prions from ground-up Scrape-infected sheep in their cattle feed.

As the food chain progressed, humans ate hamburger or other beef products and became infected with the disease. Since it was a new thought that spongiform diseases could pass from animals to humans, scientists coined a new name for the human-form of the disease - *new variant Creutzfeldt-Jakob Disease (nCJD)* .

America acted quickly. We shut the import doors to European cattle and cattle feed. Processed animal parts were banned from American cattle feeders, and we were saved from disaster in America.

However, many think the story may continue through other means. If Americans will visit their local library or their book store, they can purchase or read the Physician's Desk Reference (PDR). This book is in almost every physician's office throughout America. It is pharmaceutical information provided by Big Pharma regarding the medications the doctors prescribe for their patients every day.

As mentioned earlier, the PDR indicates that one ingredient in Merck and Company's rubella and hepatitis A vaccines is MRC-5 human aborted fetus fibroblasts. In translation, this means Americans who receive either the rubella or hepatitis A vaccines will also receive human lung cells into their blood streams.

Since scientists are unable to isolate and identify the prion before death, they can't know if a donor is infected with the disease until after the fact. Why do pharmaceutical companies want to put aborted fetus fibroblasts or any other body part into our vaccines? One reason: They are a source of protein!

Prion diseases have been transmitted through human growth hormone products, corneal grafts, and blood transfusions. In 2004, a report published in the Lancet Medical Journal showed that vCJD can be transmitted by blood transfusions *(Peden 2004)*.

The United States will not accept blood donations from persons with a cumulative total of 5 years or more of civilian travel in Western European countries (6 months or more for military if 3 months in the United Kingdom) from 1980 to 1996." *(Wikipedia Encyclopedia)*

This information poses a very important question: If prion disease can be contracted through blood, through corneal grafts, by eating the meat of an infected host, and by medical instruments, then why can't it be contracted through fetal cells?

According to some medical experts, it can!

They suggest that all human cells hold a propensity for carrying CJD. The danger not only lies in the vaccines that reportedly contain human cells, but it is also a danger in the vaccines or medications developed and manufactured in human cell substrates. The human cell substrates may or may not be reported to the public or healthcare professionals.

What about children's cancers?

According to *Childhood Cancer Foundation*, "Cancer remains the number one disease killer of America's children - more than Cystic Fibrosis, Muscular Dystrophy, Asthma and AIDS combined."

Different sources provide different reasons for the increase in childhood cancers. Some reasons include: parents who smoke, genetic predisposition, pesticides, prenatal injury, and vaccines.

When we discuss fetal cells in vaccines, we must remember the difference between fetal cells and adult cells. Fetal cells are designed to divide at an exponential rate. One small cell divides into billions and billions of cells over a nine-month period! This is their nature. This is what the coding tells them to do. They will do this in the womb, in your body, in a child's body, in a laboratory test tube.

The advantage to fetal stem cell research proponents argue is the fetal cell can become anything. It can become liver, heart, kidneys, or anything else in the body. Yes, and that may be good or that may be bad.

Controversy also permeates this area of medicine. Those who wish to inoculate us with fetal cells tell us that the teeny, teeny amount of fetal cells a person receives in an inoculation is so minute that it could do no harm.

Others say, even if there is only a minute, microscopic amount of fetal cells injected into the body, they will, in fact, do what they are designed to do– *divide exponentially.*

Now for the sake of conversation, let's include another

consideration. What if the recipient of the fetal cells had predisposition to cancer?

In Jay's case, he had a predisposition to brain cancer. He took flu shots every year for over fifteen years. If rumors are correct and the flu shot contains aborted fetal kidney cells, did these cells contribute to Jay's brain cancer? Do fetal cells divide more rapidly in children because they are children?

Do you hear them laughing? The educated, the elite, the people in the know discount me as they read. It doesn't matter. This discussion needs to take place. Right or wrong, it is Americans reactivating their brains. We are thinking for ourselves again.

We must wipe the cobwebs from our brows and halt Big Pharma's hype, admitting that our relationship with Big Pharma has deteriorated because they have deceived us, robbed us, and killed us. Think about the following information:

Big Pharma has faced *"government investigations and civil and criminal lawsuits for paying kickbacks to doctors, engaging in anticompetitive practices, colluding with generic companies to ban them from the market, illegally promoting drugs for unapproved uses, misleading the customer in direct-to-consumer advertising, and cover-up tactics"* *(Angell, M.D., 2004)*

Notice the date. These violations occurred within in the past few years. Let's examine a few of Big Pharma's deceptive tactics:

Me-Too Drugs:

"Me-Too" drugs are Big Pharma's trustworthy big money-makers. The statin drugs for lowering cholesterol are a perfect example. We may buy Mevacor, Lipitor, Pravachol, Lescol, Zocor, or Crestor.

Each of these drugs is just a variation of the others with minute changes. Manufacturers develop me-too drugs to increase prices and stretch the patent rights on a medication. It is profitable to change one molecule in a current drug, call it a new drug, raise the price of the drug, and reap benefits from the patent rights for another twenty years.

One might speculate that this is the plan for the Gardasil vaccination. Since the drug only covers four strains of the HPV virus, it would be a perfect candidate for the me-too drug.

In addition to the deception and gouging, there are two very obvious violations to the people:

First, if a person is allergic to one of these drugs or experiences an adverse reaction, doctors will very likely continue to try the rest of the drugs in that line.

Jay was one of those people. He experienced reactions with the first, the second, and the third variation of statin drugs. At that point, Jay said, "No more. I quit." We didn't know at the time that he was basically taking the same drug. If he was allergic to one of them, he was very likely allergic to all of them. However, the doctor continued to 'try' one after the other.

Secondly, while the drug companies focus on me-too drugs, they aren't finding real answers for unanswered medical issues. "Breakthroughs" are a thing of the past. Time and energy are dedicated to the me-too drugs.

The loser in me-too drugs - *All of Us!*

Finding Illnesses to Sell Drugs:

Remember the "horse urine" that would cure all women's mid-life woes? Big Pharma told us this one little pill would prevent heart problems, osteoporosis, and Alzheimer disease. They said women needed it to look young, feel young, and act young. In his book *Overdo$ed America*, Dr. Abramson dispels any doubt about Big Pharma's cynical estrogen plan.

The cure everything drug was a cure everything drug because bad news continued to plague the pill and hurt profits. They needed to find something, anything to keep the dollars rolling. Let's examine this information as reported by Dr. Abramson:

New research indicated that Hormone Replacement Therapy (HRT) increased cancer of the lining of the uterus (endometrial cancer) up to 14-fold after seven years of treatment. Subsequently, The Lancet Medical Journal later reported progestin added to the medical regimen ten days each month prevented the earlier forecast for endometrial cancer. However, the cancer scare had already taken its toll on HRT sales.

Big Pharma knew they needed an aggressive counter attack when HRT sales decreased by half. So they took the advice of one of their executive counselors when he said, "Marketing a disease is the best way to market a drug."

So they searched for a disease and osteoporosis was the winner. They began to bombard physicians throughout America with pictures and dialogue. They saturated medical journals, with visual hype including wheelchairs, x-rays of crooked spines, and women humped over with dowager's humps. They lectured; they educated; they informed.

Then their aggression became even more aggressive.

Before the marketing onslaught, approximately 23 percent of women knew about osteoporosis. So the pharmaceutical company Wyeth-Ayerst hired Burson-Marsteller, a public relations firm, to change that statistic.

They filled women's magazines with graphics and articles about the disease. Soon everyone knew about osteoporosis, including men, women and children. The drug companies provided financial support to help found the National Osteoporosis Foundation.

The drug company spent millions of dollars and the goal was accomplished. The American women were thinking osteoporosis rather than endometrial cancer. Ironically, at about the same time, the Framingham Heart Study published an article in the New England Journal of Medicine warning that HRT raised women's likelihood of heart disease more than fifty times.

Propaganda trumped the study. America was too wrapped up in the hype. The heart study went unheeded. Big Pharma's massive propaganda campaign worked. Premarin sales became greater than before the cancer scare. One out of five women took HRT.

Trusted academia joined in 'pushing' the agenda. The American College of Physicians said, "all women . . . should consider preventive hormone therapy for 10 to 20 years." The American College of Obstetrics and Gynecology recommended all postmenopausal women should take HRT for life! HRT use increased 30 percent over the next three years.

Finally, American women learned the truth. The Women's Health Initiative revealed HRT did not prevent Alzheimer disease, *it doubled the risk.* HRT did not prevent heart disease; it *increased the risk 50 times.* HRT increased breast cancer, heart attack, stroke, and blood clots. *(Abramson, 2005)*

The stakes were high, the expenses were high, Big Pharma's financial rewards were high. Deception was over the top!

Who were the losers? - - - - *America's Women*

Epidemic Iatrogenesis

We feel energetic; we feel good; we are having a good day. Then we begin to hear the message that others don't think we look so well. The voices nag at us all day:

"Is everything okay? You look terrible." "Gosh, were you up all night?" "You look bushed." "Why do you have dark circles under your eyes?" "You look warm. Do you have a temperature?"

At the end of the day, we are sick. We don't know why, but our body tells us we are ill. This is what happens every time America turns on the television set. Big Pharma is there, raising its ugly head, saying: "You are not well, your sex life is sooo boring, your ten-year-old daughter is having sex, you don't have any get-up-and-go, where is your glow?"

We are hooked, without knowing the truth, without knowing the plan. We forget the stories of HRT, Vioxx, Bextra, Estrogen and more. We agree with it, we buy it, we accept part of the story as planned.

Then it happens. The real pain begins. Our stomachs hurt; our heads hurt, our kidneys quit; our blood pressure fluctuates; we feel dizzy, dehydrated, and shaky. We go to the doctor again. He prescribes more medicine, more shots, and extended prescription time.

We are on a roll, when a glass of orange juice, an aspirin, a run in the park, or a flip on the television switch would have helped us so much more.

Let's put this concept into real time. Big Pharma advertizes that Pravachol and other statin drugs may reduce strokes. However, even though they quickly list them in television commercials, they don't elaborate on the possible iatrogenic illnesses. Pravachol may cause many iatrogenic illnesses, including hives, back pain, muscle pain, cramps and worse.

However, if we searched and found the rest of the information, we would learn that controlling our blood pressure will reduce our chances of stroke by 35 to 45 percent. Or even better yet, two hours of moderate exercise will reduce our chance of stroke by a whopping 60 percent! *(Abramson, 2005)*

Limited information is the same as false information if the informer gives only a partial account of what he knows. Therefore, when Big Pharma presents drug information with a pretence to help, but fails to inform about side-effects or other more affordable, more natural, solutions, the information becomes lies, pure and simple!

We shouldn't listen to the commercials. We shouldn't ask our doctor to give us this drug or that drug. That is what Big Pharma is banking on - - - all the way to the cashier. We should go to our doctors and say instead, "I don't want the drug that is the newest 'kid on the block'. I want a time-tested and trusted medication at the lowest dose to do the job. If there is a natural remedy, that is even better yet!"

Who is hurt by Big Pharma's lies? . . . . .*All of Us*

Monopolizing the Market

Hairdressers, social workers, and teachers all must continue to learn innovations in their fields. They get together, study, and improve their skills. However, that diligence may not apply to our doctors, those who have our lives in their hands. According to some reports, doctors' continuing education has fallen by the wayside.

"That is not true," one may argue. "They are required to attend seminars, lectures, and continuing education too. Their state medical licenses depend upon hours in these academic endeavors."

However, we must acknowledge that participation does not guarantee pertinent information. As state-of-the-art healthcare has become a dream of the past, with termination trumping rehabilitation, so has the caliber of doctor training.

According to Abramson, "The medical industry (mainly Big Pharma) funded 70 percent of all continuing education for doctors in 2003." Now it doesn't take a brain surgeon to calculate the probability of agenda changes with Big Pharma in the lead!

Drs. Arnold Relman and Marcia Angell said yesterday's "sober professionalism of a few decades ago" at doctors' continuing education meetings had declined to "trade-show hucksterism."

Big Pharma is intent on widening its follower base and showering them with incentives to help guarantee loyalty to the trade. Incentives may include food, motels, trips, or anything that seems enticing at the time.

In 2000, Pfizer sponsored a meeting of leading cardiologists in Sydney, Australia, coinciding with the Olympic Games. *(Abramson, 2005)*

It is estimated Big Pharma spent $25.3 billion in 2003, which included free samples, meals, conference fees, air fares, and continuing education. Big Pharma denies any coercion on their part. They contend the gifts are given out of the goodness of their hearts and that they have no impact on the doctors' prescribing habits. *(Tady, 2007)*

"The drug industry doesn't spend $20 or $30 billion a year on advertising prescription drugs unless they believe it has an impact on doctors prescribing," said Dr. Sidney Wolfe, director of Public Citizen's Health Research Group.

"You would probably like to know whether your doctor is getting no money, some money, a lot of money, or a huge amount of money, because it's going to influence what that doctor decides for you." Also, if the physicians' gifts mean nothing, then 'prescription tracking' wouldn't be necessary.

However, Big Pharma purchases pharmacy records to identify what doctors write the most prescriptions. Then the doctors are numbered from one to ten, placing the high-prescribing doctors in the number one and two slots. This information is financially necessary for strategically placing profit-yielding gifts in the community. *(Adams, 2007)*

Who does this financial arrangement hurt? . . ..*All of Us.*

Money Earmarked for Corruption

The FDA's first and foremost job is to protect the American public. However, their incestuous relationship with Big Pharma is putting Americans at risk rather than providing a blanket of security.

Dr. David Graham, senior drug safety researcher at the FDA, documented FDA's failure to protect the American people when he testified before the Senate Finance Committee, informing the world of FDAs inaction regarding the deadly drug Vioxx.

The following information was gleaned from Dr. Graham's testimony before the U.S. Senate Finance Committee:

Even though FDA exists to protect the American people, the agency is dedicated to protecting industry's interests above everything else. FDA views industry as its client. Dr. Graham said, "*As currently configured, the FDA is not able to adequately protect the American public.*"

The FDA resource breakdown is:

Drug Safety	**5%**
Other	**20%**
Drug Approval	**80%**

The "gorilla in the living room" is new drug approval. Congress has not only created that structure, they have also worsened that structure through the Prescription Drug User Fee Act, by which drug companies pay money to the FDA so they will review and approve its drug. Dr. Graham explains.

The FDA cooperates with Big Pharma's agenda to put new drug approval on the fast track. Profit is the bottom line and every minute wasted is money lost. That is one reason me-too drugs are so profitable.

They can change one molecule quickly and approval is swift.

There are many classes of drugs where we've got 10 or 15 members of that class. They all lower your blood pressure. They all lower your cholesterol. Another one comes along and the FDA feels its obligation to approve it. . . . .Currently, the way the incentives are for industry, it's safer to do a "me too" drug, another drug in the same class." Dr. Graham said.

Dr. Graham describes the financial arrangement between the two power-houses: *The drug companies pay a substantial amount of money to the FDA at the time that they bring a drug application for approval in order for the FDA to review the drug. Basically it's a tax. It's a fee. Industry pays the fee, and the FDA will review the drug application. But the real expectation is from the company: "We've paid our money, now approve our drug." That's basically how the FDA reacts as well.*

Dr. Graham advises that the FDA should be independent of the industry it regulates. When there is money-changing between two institutions the dynamics change. Money influences behavior, readjusting incentives and outcomes. Dr. Graham said, *"Industry money is influencing the decisions that get made, and it creates this incentive structure . . . . the FDA is unduly influenced by industry and that undue influence is in part the result of industry money funding the FDA operations.*

Dr. Graham has told his story. He has exposed the lies, but he can't do it alone. Big Pharma is unrestrained. Their 'rap sheet' is long. They are a powerhouse that will take a huge force to stop. If they don't push their way, they buy their way. Whistle blowers, like Dr. Graham, have tried to stop them, doctors have tried to stop them, individual legislators have tried to stop them. The only ones with the real power to stop them are *YOU* and *ME*.

When we, the American people, get smart, when we realize the pickpocket has our wallet, when we know everything that comes out of their mouths (reports, commercials, official and unofficial statements) is said purely for the sake of profit, when we evaluate our health *after* we take the drug against our health *before* the drug, when we quit trusting the thief, the liar, the perpetrator, we will take action.

We will ring our legislator's phones off the hooks. We will refuse to buy into the commercial hype. We will tell our doctors we want the most tried and trusted medication on the shelf.

We will investigate alternative medicine and we will drink juice, walk, exercise, relax, eat healthy and shun the pill.

Part 3:

The Third Reich in America

Parallel Thinking - Third Reich with America
The last time this combination of forces worked in concert,
over 200,000 individuals lost their lives in Nazi, Germany,
even before the final solution. Most of these persons were
German citizens sacrificed for medical reasons set by economic
and social agendas. I find the parallels chilling. (Linda Peeno,
Congressional Testimony, 1996)

When Jay passed away and I emerged from the trenches in the white-coat war zone emotionally battered, bruised, and bleeding, I believed the Third Reich was in America today – now! But kind voices, gentle voices, came to me and asked me to look around.

That is when I saw them, brave men, women, and children still fighting the fight. The number was more than a few, so I began to count. Concerned Women of America, Jay Sekulow, Physicians for Life, the Heritage Foundation, Alliance for Human Research Protection, James Dobson, National Vaccine Information Center and so many more.

So I began to refocus, looking at parallel thinking, the Third Reich with America, and the timely warnings for us to stay alert, demand accountability, and face the giants without reserve.

This is what emerged for me to explore:

- Disposable Lives
- Perverted Medicine
- Accountability Crises
- Unrestrained Power
- Deceptions on the Loose
- Dead Silence

Third Reich – American Precedent or Detergence?
The Holocaust happened to all who missed the Nazi 'mark' of perfection. (Brandi Newman)

As we examine the six areas of parallel thinking – the Third Reich with America – we will see the dangerous slippery slope America is treading. We will read words of retrospective wisdom, of warnings, and prophetic counsel from those who have studied the Third Reich deep, down inside each filthy little cranny.

Then the question must be answered. Will America choose to listen, using the words to muster will and ambition, cleansing a dirty, foul system from our land or will we choose to turn our heads and turn our attention, sticking to loose ambition, running the opposite direction, delegating action, burying our heads in the sand as the system entraps us?

Disposable Lives – Doctors were quickly assimilated into the system, giving their efforts to the cause. "Doctors joined the Nazi party earlier and in greater numbers than any other profession," Dr. Robert N. Proctor wrote.

Mercy killings began in nursing homes and mental institutions. Doctors evaluated the person's health using a questionnaire. Then the lives he determined 'worth living' were spared. Those who didn't measure up to his standards were condemned with the stroke of the pen. The doctor placed a plus (+) in their paper work as the sign they were doomed to die!

Dr. Leo Alexander said the thought that some don't have "life worthy to be lived" marked the starting point for the tyranny of the Third Reich.

Then Social Darwinism, in concert with politicized medicine, provided the rationale for legitimizing the elite, the powerful, and the rich making life/death decisions for all.

So the question for America remains: If the name of the game is survival of the fittest, who should make the 'mark - +', doctors, and lawyers, and politicians, and friends of those with the pen?

In accordance with the research I conducted, it is my belief that without the willing participation of a large part of the German medical establishment, the Holocaust could not have taken place. (Fishkoff, 1996)

Perverted Medicine – The Nazi doctors continued to raze human dignity, rights, and lives, flaunting pseudoscience as justifiable cause to violate and annihilate those with the mark under the safety of the Gestapo mob.

The Nazi physicians gathered subjects from concentration camps to see what would happen to human beings when they were confined to a low atmosphere environment. They forced them into pressure chambers until their lungs exploded. *(Silverstein, 1996)*

Nazi physicians needed a way to compare various vaccines. So they inoculated inmates with malaria, typhus, smallpox, cholera, and spotted fever. *(Silverstein, 1991)*

Nazi doctors operated on subjects without anesthesia. *(Silverstein, 1996)*

The Law for the Prevention of Genetically Diseased Offspring made it possible for Nazi doctors to perform forced sterilization on approximately 400,000 men and women.

How did this happen? What swooped doctors into pretend science and mutilation of the masses?

It was the "...German doctors' initial bending of their Hippocratic Oath during the 'mercy killing' program, (which led) to their final moral collapse when called upon to give a spurious medical 'aura' to the mass exterminations .. " (Fishkoff, 1996)

Accountability Crises – The Nazi doctors reveled in their madness. Dr. Hans Munch, who participated in unrestrained atrocities at Auschwitz, later described the experience as fascinating. Others claimed the euthanasia program was a "better good". It was good for society, for medicine, and for science! *(Tanantola, 1993)*

"Hitler mesmerized the German people," said Alexander Kimel, a Holocaust survivor.

And so the stage was set. A broken people, needing resurrection, chose to follow a man of lies. Boundaries were removed, moral codes were released, personal discretion ceased and people began to die.

Therein lies the danger. When a broken people willfully surrender their voices, their discretions, their all to another, it depletes their personal resources, making them sterile, unable to change the consequences of their actions.

Unrestrained Power – *The people's adoration, trust, and unrestrained following spurred Hitler into greater depths as he revealed in his own egomaniacal wonders. (Kimel)*

Everything fell into place. Hitler was untouchable, his followers were inexorable, and the Gestapo was brutal. Speakers could no longer speak and the protestors could no longer protest. The lock was set and it could only be opened through ruin or release. So the people waited oppressed.

Deceptions on the Loose – Deception depends upon masking an undesirable reality. Those who are masters of the lie instinctively know what to disclose and what to withhold. Hitler gained his world-leader position through this manipulation.

"He was a cauldron of contradictions. . . .He was charming or brutal, generous or savage." *(Lutzer, 1995)*

According to Lutzer, Hitler convinced the masses of his peaceful intentions as he prepared for war. He befriended then assassinated. He bragged about his honesty as he deceived.

That which is false, that which can fool the masses will be guised as hype, propaganda, euphuisms and others. It will take the discerning, those who believe in their own autonomy, to stop the deceitful march by discovering the reality in the rhetoric.

Dead Silence – The German churches adopted blind-eye and deaf ear philosophies. The Third Reich mentality marched forward. Hitler banned prayers in the schools. He robbed Christian holidays, mandating they morph into new meaning, with new names and new reasons. The churches abandon the people and their calling, falling before a false king, accepting the ideology, the actions, and the new reality.

When the churchmen awoke from their spiritual and political slumbers, they discovered too late that they had been deceived. (Lutzer, 1995)

Third Reich Descriptions

We took such a small glimpse, such a teeny-tiny view, yet we saw the horror, the devastation, and the tyranny too. With the Third Reich in mind, let's take a look at America. How do we compare?

Can we see it? Can we hear it? Will we heed the warnings and do something about them? Let's examine it and see . . . . . will the Third Reich story become a precedent or a detergence for America today.

Disposable Lives

Science is outrunning the human spirit; man is becoming obsolete. A 'brave new world' hovers in the wings of man and of our civilization. But it is no golden age. It is merely the old tyranny resuscitated by an inhumane science. (Whitehead, 1983)

Euthanasia is on the move in America. In 2001, the Hospice Patient's Alliance reported: *the U.S. Office of Inspector General and state enforcement agencies confirmed hospitals and doctors fraudulently moved chronically ill patients into hospice settings.*

Doctors referred patients to hospice because they provided an income source. However, when the individuals depleted their financial resources, hospice put them to death. Families' reported hospice staff falsified medical records.

Euthanasia was accomplished by sedating the patient to death. Over-sedation causes a medically-induced coma. The patient dies because his breathing is shut-down by a lethal narcotic over-dose, like morphine. Sometimes the patient dies of dehydration while in the prolonged coma state. They call this "terminal sedation." *(Hospice Patient Alliance)*

Reportedly two-thirds of U.S. physicians support physician assisted suicide, and America has an established protocol for euthanasia. Ironically, it is called the *Third Path.*

According to the marketing and advertising research company's press release, reprinted in nearly a dozen health journals including, *Mental Health Weekly, Pharma Law Weekly, Life Science Weekly,* and *Physician Law Weekly*, the term "*Third Path*" translates to "*Patient Termination*" in America.

Third Path status alerts America's medical staff that the patient is on a 'hasten death protocol.' The Third Path is the order to remove anything that might sustain life, including food, water, and antibiotics. It may also provide the green light for sedation to the point of termination.

Many reports indicate that Advance Directives provide no protection against the euthanasia onslaught.

When the language used in living wills was analyzed, the conclusion was that the wording is specifically designed to support the third path initiative. Nearly half the states' legislators approved the terminology in living wills.

Other states have laws that clearly forbid doctors from removing life sustaining supports from the patient without the patient's or his family's permission.

It was my understanding that Missouri was one of the states that does not allow doctors to withhold life-sustaining nutrition from a patient without his or his family's consent.

In the heat of argument over providing nutritional support for my husband, one nurse reiterated this belief. She said, "Missouri law is very clear that we may not remove food and water from a patient's medical protocol without the family's permission."

I researched. Multiple internet sites, both for and against euthanasia, stated that before life sustaining supports may be removed from patients in Missouri "there must be specific evidence that an incompetent patient would want treatment withdrawn."

Jim, another gentleman in another hospital, asked to remain on the ventilator. The request was notarized and placed in an official document. Medical staff suddenly began to administer morphine and Ativan.

Jim became so intoxicated on drugs he could no longer speak for himself and nurses began delivering the 'death speak.' "He's not in there. He can't make decisions any longer. He can't think." The family became suspicious.

As I did with Jay, the family forbade any further use of narcotics, restoring Jim to his prior level of functioning. Again, Jim could express his wishes in his own words.

Another family was not so fortunate. Their family member was in the very early stages of Alzheimer disease. He had recently received a thorough medical examination. His heart, kidneys, and other vital organs were deemed in good shape. There were no other pressing medical issues. He was scheduled to move into a long-term care setting the next day.

He never made it. He died in the night. The hospital told the family their loved one miraculously died of a heart attack. The family didn't believe it. Later, they learned that nurses gave the patient a 'relaxer' to calm his anxiety in the middle of the night.

Dr. John LaPuma said "The real danger of advance directives in managed care is that they will be used to limit needed, useful expensive treatment under the guise of ethics." in his article *Advance Directives in Managed Care: Are They Inspired by Love or Money?*

David Gibbs, attorney for Bob and Mary Schindler in the Terri Schiavo case advocates "Designation of Health Care Surrogate(s)". The surrogate designation is a legal paper naming an individual or individuals who will honor the person's end-of-life wishes, speaking for him when he is unable to speak for himself.

Mr. Gibbs writes: "The laws governing healthcare surrogates may vary from state to state." In his book, *Fighting for Dear Life*, he provides a form as a starting point for persons and their attorneys to develop surrogate designation. However, since state laws differ, a person may want to contact legal advice in his state.

Designating a surrogate eliminates the possibility of dying from an automobile accident because the living will indicates the person doesn't want to be put on a respirator. A more informed decision can be made at the time of injury. The respirator may only be needed for a short time until the patient heals enough to breathe on his own again. Premature death due to a piece of paper that can't judge circumstances is a travesty.

It is difficult to comprehend how we Americans can divide ourselves. We review and revisit the Third Reich sickness and wickedness and horror with clear pictures of the atrocities, yet we fail to see the *Third Path* in our own modern hospital corridors.

Perverted Medicine

In Nazi Germany, "A perversion of medicine occurred in the more traditional settings of the medical clinic, the chronic care institution, the university hospital and academia among the mainstream of physicians." (Shevell)

America has been struggling against pseudoscience and pseudo-medicine for many years. These phenomena are perverted medicine in the first degree, calling for 'life' sacrifices to feed egomaniac lusts, boost power agendas and benefit the masses.

American pseudoscience is entrenched in the social philosophy, eugenics, which is dedicated to perfecting the human being. Eugenics', born of Darwinism, is intent on creating greater intelligence and greater health among our citizens, vowing to decrease suffering and ration resources. The standards and measures used for human selection is devised by those wrapped-up in the eugenic idealism.

By the mid 1920's, 3000 people were sterilized against their will in America. Those chosen for sterilization included: orphans, people suffering epilepsy, those who were blind or deaf, individuals who scored poorly on intelligent quotient tests (IQ), and anyone deemed feebleminded by the system.

"It is better for all the world, if instead of waiting to execute degenerate offspring for crime, or let them starve for their imbecility; society can prevent those who are manifestly unfit from continuing their kind . . . . Three generations of imbeciles are enough." (Supreme Court Justice Oliver Wendell Holmes, Jr., Buck v. Bell, 1927.)

American studies designed to view death rather than save life, weed-out inferior peoples and races, and save the country from economic parasites began many years ago, but continue to march into modern time.

Examples of American pseudoscience studies include the following:

U.S.A. - Experiment/Study 1
Bad Blood - The 'Black' Man's Disease

Study Objective: How syphilis affects blacks as opposed to whites.

Theory
Whites - Experience more neurological complications

Blacks – More susceptible to cardiovascular damage

The study participants were black sharecroppers. They were poor and some couldn't read. The pseudo-scientists chose the study participants wisely, including 399 men diagnosed with syphilis and 200 others, who didn't have the disease, for their control group.

Black participants were important because they would make the study a success. The pseudo-scientists didn't want to learn how to cure syphilis, they didn't want to know how to ease the suffering from syphilis, they didn't even want to know if they could reverse its ravages; they wanted to watch how black men would die!

Since untreated syphilis "frequently led to a chronic, painful, and fatal multi-system disease", the government and university wanted to see if black men would suffer and die differently than white men. Therefore, the participants' race was essential in meeting study goals. *(Wikipedia Encyclopedia)*

The sharecroppers didn't sign any informed consent papers because they weren't informed. Informed consent would spoil the "researchers" chance to learn.

So pseudoscience forfeited personal choice for study participation by proxy. The institutions executed proprietorship over a people, and in doing so, deemed them second-class citizens.

The warped thinking continued. If they are second-class citizens and they don't know they're in a study, why do they need to know they have syphilis? So the "researchers" felt at liberty to say . . . . . "You have bad blood."

The Public Health Service Syphilis Study, or Tuskegee

Experiment, offered the men free treatment, a free ride to the clinic, one hot meal per day, and "If you die," they said, "we will pay $35 toward your funeral." Later, they became especially generous and raised the funeral benefit to $50.

By 1947, the medical community began to successfully treat syphilis with a new wonder drug called penicillin. Rapid treatment centers were set up around the nation to eradicate the disease.

This information threatened the Tuskegee experiment. If the study participants were treated and cured, the 'researchers' couldn't watch and experience *Black Death*! They couldn't meet their objectives and the study would be forced to end.

Since the sharecroppers didn't know they were in a study and they didn't know they had syphilis, they didn't need to know anything! Why would they need to know that penicillin would cure a disease they didn't know they had?

So the sharecroppers didn't receive penicillin. The 'researchers' continued to hide enlightening information as it emerged.

The Center for Disease Control (CDC) reaffirmed the need to continue the study until all subjects had died and had been autopsied, even though Peter Buxtum, a PHS Venereal Disease Investigator, expressed his concerns about the mortality rate in the experiment.

Later, under scrutiny, the pseudo-scientists still weren't repentant. They simply said the Tuskegee study participants were "all volunteers and they were always happy to see the doctors."

An Alabama state health officer added, "Somebody is trying to make a mountain out of a molehill."

Due to pseudoscience arrogance and the elite's freedom to choose *who* - 28 black men died from syphilis, 100 died from complications, 40 wives became infected, and 19 children were born with congenital syphilis! In retrospect, some of us get it now as the Wikipedia Encyclopedia explains:

"The Tuskegee Syphilis Study is often cited as one of the greatest ethical breaches of trust between physicians and patients in the setting of a clinical study in the United States."

Former President Bill Clinton presented financial restitution to the Tuskegee Syphilis Study survivors during his presidential term with these words:

The United States government did something that was wrong - deeply, profoundly, morally wrong. It was an outrage to our commitment to integrity and equality for all our citizens . . . clearly racist.

Former president Bill Clinton did the right thing. He should have apologized and paid, in the name of the people, in the name of the nation. However, the sad, sad truth is that it will take more than apology and retribution to make sure such atrocities never happen again.

U.S.A. Experiment/Study 2
Throw-Away Babies

Two groups were the plan from the beginning. One was group A, the other was group B. That is not what they called them, but that is what we will call them at this time, for this purpose.

Group A and Group B were similar in some ways. Both groups were parents. Both had babies suffering from spina bifida. Both groups loved their babies. Most of them were good parents or tried to be. They all strived to work, to play, to live as well as possible. They were all seeking the same thing -- help for their babies. They didn't know anything was awry. They didn't know they were in a group. They were just there -- seeking.

The group had some differences in other ways. The parents in Group A were poor. Many were called minorities by the people who lived across the way. They had difficulty making ends meet. Many received money from others for their medical care. They struggled, from time to time, buying their groceries and paying their bills.

Parents in Group B were not poor. Their lives reflected financial order. They paid for medical insurance, and cars, vacations, and television and more.

So money was the main difference between Group A and

Group B. It didn't just happen that way. It was actually in the scheme of things. Four doctors and a social worker were there. Let's *imagine* what they might have said.

"Let's divide the parents into two groups. Let's put the poor parents over here in this group. Put those who are able to pay over there."

"Then we can find out," they said, "if parents in group A will forfeit their baby's treatment and put them to rest! We'll treat the babies in group B, giving them the best that we have. Our ultimate goal is to prove a theory: *Group A Parents will listen to us and choose the "Third path."*

Since the federal government agreed to pay for the experiment, they knew the plan. The four doctors and a social worker knew the plan. The Oklahoma University School of Medicine knew the plan too. It was only those people assigned to Group A and Group B who didn't know the plan.

So parents in Group A were marked, *Pessimistic Group*, or in layman's terms - Babies' Death Group. Parents in Group B were marked, *Optimistic Group*, or Babies' Life Group.

Then they sat down and wrote the two sets of scripts. They laid out the plan. They practiced the dialogue and then began. Always delivering. Always persuading. Never overtly. Always covertly.

We can imagine the pessimistic conversation went like this:

Group A: Your little girl will never recover no matter what we do. We just can't fix her disability. You will have to care for her the rest of her life. She may be blind too. It is too bad that she will never know you. She may resemble an animal more than a human being.

The optimistic conversation may have sounded like this:

Group B: We can operate on your child. The failure rate for this surgery is very low. We almost always get good results. The operation will improve his sensory, mobility, and intellectual abilities. His chances for a productive, enjoyable life are positive.

The plan was executed. The criteria were met. Parents listened to their trusted doctors and the experiment was a success. *Twenty-four babies were buried.*

This is a matter-of-fact presentation of the case, using documented information in story format. It depicts the ease, the casualness in which violations against the poor and weak are formulated and executed. It is real life of it! It is the Third Reich of it!

The following information regarding the spina bifida experiment process was gleaned from the following: articles in the *New York Post* and the *Alliance for Human Research Protection;* Jamie Doran's award winning documentary *Guinea Pig Kids.*

"If you have a family limited financially, emotionally and sometimes geographically, you're going to have to make compromises," one of the researchers said in defense of the medical teams experimental strategies.

This statement provides great insight into the researchers world view. If we consider that the experimental goal was to procure the death of 24 babies, we *experience* the researchers words rather than hear them. The context deepens, the message changes, the implications frighten.

The *Experiential Truth* of the researchers' statement becomes*:*

> *I will decide how much money you must make. I will decide if poor tears differ from rich tears, if poor problems differ from rich problems.*
>
> *I elect myself authority over you. If you can't satisfy my financial criteria, then you can't make family medical decisions on your own. I will obliterate that right in the name of society, in the name of medicine.*
>
> *I will take up the authority, reigning over information dissemination, outcome possibilities, and your autonomy. I will decide!*

And decide they did! No medical criteria were established for the spina bifida experiment. They weren't trying to determine a better way of treating spina bifida. They didn't want to know how to better support families who had children suffering from spina bifida. They didn't want to discover better intervention strategies.

They wanted to know, if through medical suggestion and through trusted physicians' opinions, parents would allow their babies to die.

They expressed the plan for group selection, *Pessimistic* or *Optimistic*, in a mathematical equation: $QL=NE \times (H+S)$.

QL equals quality of life. NE equals the parents' natural endowment, both physical and intellectual. H+S equals the sum of the contribution from home, family and society.

The five-member doctor experimental team listed the following quality of life considerations as some of the factors used in selecting families for the "allow to die" group.

➢ The parents "economic and intellectual" resources.

➢ The potential for the child to live outside a wheelchair.

➢ The child's 'suspected' level of retardation.

➢ A social agency's commitment to provide rehabilitation.

One of the researchers elaborated "We described the process that I think is a good one . . . virtually all of the babies that were treated survived and virtually all of the ones who had no treatment died."

It is true that all babies treated survived, except one who died in a car wreck, and all those who didn't receive treatment died. However, the researcher's statement didn't mention the fact that eight families denied the doctors' recommendation for non-treatment.

These families "vigorously" demanded that doctors treat their babies. Six babies, designated for death by the medical team, survived. Doctors termed one of the survivors as "robust and thriving." The remaining children moved out of state with their parents.

The 24 babies designated for death were transferred to Oklahoma Children's Shelter. The shelter was federally funded, but didn't have a license.

They were not equipped to care for the very ill. The facility didn't administer sedatives, antibiotics, or other medications to the babies, and all died within 189 days. Most deaths were attributed to acute infections and respiratory distress.

Many families in the optimistic group revered the doctors until they discovered they had been in an experiment without their permission. Suddenly the doctors who saved their babies were no longer held in esteem.

The *Washington Post* reported that *one of the researchers acknowledged that 10 of the 24 children who died as a result of the selection process "would have survived" if they had been treated, but he said, 'family' considerations prompted a recommendation for non-treatment.*

"The doctors are there to heal, not to make qualitative decisions about where someone might be in 10 years. They have the skill to operate. . . . so operate. Treat the baby. That's all we parents ask. Give us the burden, and let people take care of their own lives," said Mrs. Veronica Donnelly, a parent of a child in the experiment group.

"No committee of doctors could predict how I would adjust to that because I didn't know and Fred (her husband) didn't know how he was going to adjust to it," Mrs. Donnelly continued.

Litigation ensued. The doctors won. They were not held accountable.

The "good process of *selection*" they designed is used by doctors and hospitals every day in 2007. Jay and I experienced the same dialogue directed to the pessimistic group.

This experience suggests that Jay was repeatedly placed in the *Third Path*, the 'to die group', without our knowledge and without our permission.

U.S.A. Example Study/Experiment 3 -
May 2005

Sacrificial Lambs

On March 10, 2004, they made it public.

"The Alliance for Human Research Protection filed a complaint with the FDA and the Federal Office of Human Research Protection about a series of AIDS drugs experiments conducted on New York children in foster care."

The Federal Government and the Office of Human Research Protection, OHRP, initiated investigations. The Associated Press (AP) and British Broadcasting Company (BBC) also began journalistic inquiries.

New York was not alone. Illinois, Louisiana, Maryland, North Carolina, Colorado, and Texas were also on the take. They agreed to lend their foster children infected with HIV to research.

Actually, they contended it would be a real deal. Poor, minority foster children could receive care from world-class researchers. The children would live longer and the National Institute of Health would pay the bill!

To no one's surprise, Big Pharma, made up of various pharmaceutical companies, was the National Institute of Health's partner in the sponsorship of the 'experiments'!

Big Pharma and Big Government vested in the same goal, placing vulnerable children in the highest risk, minimal safety-assurance clinical trials - Phase I and Phase II.

"The experiments were conducted on children who were wards of the state with no parents to protect them or to advocate for their best interest. These children were used as test subjects--guinea pigs--in multiple experiments testing combinations of drugs and vaccines--as many as 7 at a time," wrote *Alliance for Human Research Protection President Vera Hassner Sharav*

The BBC conducted a nine-month investigation. Their reporter Jamie Doran learned the following through interviews with the children and guardians:

> ➤ If guardians didn't want to give the prescribed medication, agencies returned the children to agency care.

> ➤ Children who refused to take the drugs were threatened.

> ➤ If children continued to refuse to take the medications, doctors inserted a peg (feeding tube) into their stomachs. Then they injected the experimental drugs directly into their intestines.

Dr. David Rasnick, HIV drug researcher at the University of Berkeley, said the drugs given to the children were "lethal." "The young aren't completely developed yet," he said. "The immune system isn't completely mature until a person's in their teens."

Among other maladies, the HIV Drugs may cause genetic mutation, organ failure, bone marrow death, bodily deformations, brain damage and fatal skin disorders.

So once the experiments began, so did the side effects. Some children developed rashes. Some experienced vomiting. Some suffered sharp drops in their infection-fighting blood cells. Some died.

Independent reports indicated two children, ages 6 and 12, suffered extreme drug toxicities resulting in strokes. Both children died, with the younger child suffering blindness before death. Others had to undergo plastic surgery to remove lumps from their necks.

According to the Alliance for Human Research Protection, at least 10 children died in the experiment testing the drug Dapsone. Four of the children died from blood poisoning.

Researchers admitted a safe, useful dosage was too difficult to determine in that particular study.

However, the researchers downplayed the death number by saying that the deaths didn't appear to be "directly attributable" to Dapsone, subsequently admitting the number of deaths in that study was "disturbing."

Controversy raged over advocacy for the children. Chicago Children's Memorial Hospital and Baltimore's Johns Hopkins University research facilities said they didn't need to provide advocates for foster kids.

However, Arthur Caplan, Department Head of Medical Ethics at the University of Pennsylvania, said, "Advocates should have been appointed for all foster children. The medications are often toxic for adults."

"There was great uncertainty as to how children would react to these AIDS medications. It is inexcusable that each child didn't have an advocate."

"Our position is that advocates weren't needed," said the spokesperson for Columbia-Presbyterian Medical Center in New York.

Illinois officials said none of the 200 foster children from their state received monitors. They reported that the document the researchers signed, which said "they would appoint an advocate for each individual ward participating in the respective medical research," was not followed.

In New York City, 142 children received monitors. However, 465 foster children were in the AIDS drug trials.

The Associated Press probe revealed that those who were old enough, between 5 and 10, gave themselves permission to participate.

Those in charge of the experiments just gave them a quick course in the risks and dangers of the study, and they made the decision all by themselves. Other times, they asked foster or biological parents; other times they didn't.

Some states didn't buy the pseudoscience hype. They removed their children from danger. They protected them with simple statements reflecting sound checks and balances in their systems.

Tennessee quickly said no thank you. "Sorry," they said, "our foster care rules prohibit enlisting children in such trials."

California pulled back too. "Such action would require a judge's order in our state," they said.

And Wisconsin responded with an emphatic nay! "Wisconsin has absolutely never allowed, nor would we even consider, any clinical experiments with the children in our foster care system," said Stephanie Marquis, spokeswoman for Wisconsin's foster care.

These children without voices were the children Big Pharma and Big Government deemed capable to decide if the experiment objectives were in their own best interests.

Some voices did speak for the children, however. Following the award-winning documentary filmmaker, Jamie Doran's, BBC documentary, "Guinea Pig Kids," which aired in December 2004, protests were organized.

The documentary spoke of the relationship among the Agency for Children's Services, the Catholic Archdiocese of New York, GlaxoSmithKline, and the National Institute of Health that allowed lethal experimental medicines be given to Black and Latino minors infected with HIV."

American pharmaceutical companies were also mentioned as participants in the sordid HIV experiments, including Pfizer and Merck and Company, the maker of the Gardasil vaccine.

The efforts of the BBC and the AP provided some information, some awareness for the public. However, medical privacy laws protected research and foster care agencies, allowing them to remain mum.

They refused to provide further information. They wouldn't disclose drug dosages. They wouldn't give full details of side effects. They wouldn't disclose the total number of deaths. And for some reason, foster parents and the children who participated in the drug trials subsequently were unavailable for interviews.

These children were violated. Pseudoscience was protected.

Some have lamented, "Too bad white collar crime doesn't have the same statutes as street crime. If it did, we could call this a "cold case," take it back off the shelves, investigate the deaths and make applicable prosecution and restitution."

The AIDS studies generated financial rewards for the institutions involved in the experiments. Their financial gain also was undisclosed.

Alliance for Human Research Protection, AHRP is a national network of lay people and professionals dedicated to advancing responsible and ethical medical research practices, to ensure that human rights and dignity and welfare of human subjects are protected, and to minimize the risks associated with such endeavors.

Accountability Crises

It is the first responsibility of every citizen to question authority.
(Benjamin Franklin)

In each of the pseudoscience studies just described, we experienced the violation of a people, the devaluing of life, the selective criteria of the elite, including government, academia, and medicine.

When thought is perverted, when accountability is forfeited, when the elite prevail without restraint, we find the sacrificed become the poor, the sick, the elderly, the disabled, and those deemed an undesirable race.

Today, in America, bending or discrediting the Hippocratic Oath is a ploy to provide greater leverage for the medical caretaker.

Too many doctors advocate killing the elderly, the feeble, the sick because they don't have "quality of life". They use the Hippocratic Oath only in the context of serving their own personal agendas.

The "quote" from the Hippocratic Oath that doctors continually threw at Jay and I over and over again was: "I must first do no harm."

Besides being a statement packed with subjective connotations, it is a direct misquote. The original statement implies much more and when viewed in full context actually contradicts the doctors misquote.

The Oath actually states: *"I will abstain from harming or wronging any man"* When *or wronging* is added to the statement, it changes the entire concept and indicates the doctors were violating the very quote they were professing to follow.

Jay was wronged when he was dumped on home health. He was wronged when doctors refused to care for him or refer him. He was wronged when no one came to his aid and he suffered septic shock. He was wronged when his bladder was bulging with urine. He was wronged when they over-sedated him and he fell, suffering injury. And all this pain and suffering was endured under the pretence "I must first do no harm!"

The original Hippocratic Oath was black and white in meaning. It left no squeeze-room for personal agendas.

Anthropologist Margaret Mead wrote these words in regard to the Hippocratic Oath:

> *For the first time in our tradition there is a complete separation between killing and curing. Throughout the primitive world, the doctor and the sorcerer tended to be the same person. He with the power to kill had the power to cure, including specially the undoing of his own killing activities.*
>
> *He who had the power to cure would necessarily also be able to kill.*
>
> *. . . With the Greeks the distinction was made clear, one profession, the followers of Asclepius, were to be dedicated completely to life under all circumstances regardless of rank, age, or intellect - the life of a slave, the life of the Emperor, the life of a foreign man, the life of a defective child . . "*

A study conducted in 150 American and Canadian medical schools revealed the following information regarding modern versions of the Hippocratic Oath: only 14% forbade euthanasia, 8% prohibited abortion, and 3% forbade sexual contact with patients.

Euthanasia, abortion, and sexual contact with patients were all forbidden in the original Hippocratic Oath. *(Farlander, 2003)*

❖ *I will not give a fatal draught to anyone if I am asked, nor will I suggest any such thing.*

❖ *Neither will I give a woman means to procure an abortion.*

❖ *I will not abuse my position to indulge in sexual contacts with the bodies of women or of men, whether they are freemen or slaves.*

Considering these three statements, it is not difficult to understand why many modern American doctors don't subscribe to the original Hippocratic Oath. Therefore, when a doctor throws out the statement, "I must first do no harm," Americans should turn and refute the statement, knowing it is pure, unadulterated garbage!

As we view this information in the context of the three studies cited earlier, listening to the excuses, rationalizations, and self-adoration following the atrocities, we see America is failing to hold the healthcare system accountable!

- ✓ *The men were all volunteers and they were happy to see the doctors.*

- ✓ *Someone is trying to make a mountain out of a molehill.*

- ✓ *Our position was that advocates weren't needed for the children.*

- ✓ *Children between the ages of 5-10 are old enough to advocate for themselves.*

- ✓ *We designed a good process of selection.*

Add to this information the story of the doctors, nurses, hospital aids, and other staff who continued to walk around the dying patient in the California hospital as she screamed for help until she died. . . . authorities ruled it "*accidental death*"!

America is not immune. America has not learned the lesson. Our slippery-slide into pseudoscience is not in the distant future, it is not in the near future. It is now!

Remember the quote: *In accordance with the research I conducted, it is my belief that without the willing participation of a large part of the German 'medical establishment', the Holocaust could not have taken place. (Fishkoff, 1996)*

Unrestrained Power

Nearly all men can stand adversity, but if you want to test a man's character, give him power. (Abraham Lincoln)

Power and the drive for ethnic purity were two forces that pushed Germany toward the Holocaust. Money is the driving force in America. Power and 'survival of the fittest' are also key players in America's downward march. However, the ultimate 'honey' that attracts non-players into the death-player role is money.

I knew a farmer years ago who raised a few pigs. He didn't have today's modern pig-raising setup, so the hog shed had a very foul odor. The workers complained about the smell every time they helped the sows birth piglets or when they had to spend an extended period of time cleaning the hog shed. So the farmer teased them about the smell. He would pick up a newly born piglet, afterbirth still attached, hold it up for all to see, take a deep whiff, and say, "Mmmmm. Money!"

This scenario describes what some healthcare professionals in America are doing today. They sidestep the foul odor emitted from negligence, withdrawal of services, and death by concentrating on the money that will result. Cash dividends put smiles on their faces as people die around them.

Medical Schizophrenia - split personality - is another phenomenon that plagues America's healthcare world.

Medical Schizophrenia allows perpetrators to disassociate themselves from their death-mongering but allows them to reap the monetary rewards and self-invented noble causes. This pivot can only occur when one rationalizes his world in two disconnected realms.

In each pseudoscience study cited earlier, the doctors, the government, the child care agencies, and others involved disconnected these two world spheres.

In the face of documented deaths and suffering, they expounded on their "good works," showing pride and satisfaction in their blind, self-determined noble contributions to humanity.

Deaths in America continue to mount under this same truth-bending, pretense. An estimated 106,000 people die in America each year due to adverse reactions to prescription drugs. *(Montague, 2007)*

Poisoning from prescription drugs is the second-largest cause of unintentional deaths in the United States, according to the federal Centers for Disease Control and Prevention. *(Whitney, 2007*

Deceptions on the Loose

The great enemy of the truth is very often not the lie - - deliberate, contrived, and dishonest - - but the myth - - persistent, persuasive, and unrealistic. (John F. Kennedy)

He was a popular guy. He had the talent to draw others to him, the ability to capture their will to follow, and the finesse to keep them loyal no matter the task. He was a leader in the true sense.

He was a master orator and manipulator. He spoke his mind with a come-hither "carrot and stick" manner. He led the people. He led them into madness, barbarism, destruction, and annihilation. And they *chose* to follow! His name was . . . Hitler.

It is amazing that the American government makes law to save the unborn child from violent crime, but funds an industry that mutilates this same child in the mother's womb. It doesn't have to make sense; it just has to make money.

Planned Parenthood, in America has a strong lobbying faction, providing big dollars to legislative campaigns and other government officials. Over the last two years, Planned Parenthood, America's number one abortion provider, has reaped the benefits of its labor, receiving more than $500 *million* in taxpayer money through Title X. *(Jay Sekulow, Chief Counsel, ACLJ)*

Think about it, America! *Your legislature gives more rights to eagles' fertilized eggs than to your daughter's, your sister's, or your own. If you snuff out the life of a snail in Wisconsin, you may be jailed and fined $10,000. (Dew, Milwaukee Journal, 1992)*

Yet, in the name of "choice," your offspring, your children's children, the heirs of your genealogical estate may be sliced and diced for a price.

Listen, America! Does Planned Parenthood say what you thought they said? Do your elected representatives say what you thought they said? Listen again.

Margaret Sanger, founder of Planned Parenthood was a racist, a dissenter, and a fugitive. She wrote for a Socialist Party publication and founded a paper called *The Woman Rebel.*

She believed a woman's 'choice' trumped all others' choices -- the father's, the families', the community's, the nation's.

Women's 'choice' advocates sex without responsibility; it advocates for others, the community, the nation to responsibly fund her irresponsibility.

Sanger's own words testify to the charges made against her. She said:

"The most merciful thing that a large family does to one of its infant members is to kill it."
(Eugenics Publ. Co. 1920,1923)

"Couples should be required to submit applications to have a child."
(Birth Control Review, 1932)

On blacks, immigrants and indigents:
" . . human weeds, "reckless breeders" . . .human beings who never should have been born."
(Pivot of Civilization)

Women's 'choice' snuffed out the lives of *over 40 million American babies from* 1973 to 2001 at a cost of multi-*billion* dollars, grief, loss, psychological trauma.

Devastation pours upon the American taxpayer, young women, men, and families throughout America, and all to satisfy the power-lust of one industry as American legislative bodies lay prone before it.

The following information chronicles Planned Parenthood's legacy:

Planned Parenthood is trying to bring sex education programs and abortion counseling into churches, calling its programs "faith-based initiatives." (7/27/02, *World*).

Planned Parenthood also receives a set percentage of total United Way campaign funds. *(George Grant, Grand Illusions)*

Only an extreme amount of corruption in both political parties could explain how Planned Parenthood gets over $300 million in tax dollars year after year.

"Abortion is the number-one killer of blacks in America," says Rev. Johnny Hunter of LEARN. *"We're losing our people at the rate of 1,452 a day. That's just pure genocide. There's no other word for it. [Sanger's] influence and the whole mindset that Planned Parenthood has brought into the black community ... say it's okay to destroy your people. We bought into the lie; we bought into the propaganda."*

America lives a Schizophrenic existence under Planned Parenthood's dictatorship. We call our murdered babies fetuses, embryos, zygotes, cellular masses. We don't call them - babies.

Photographs of the destruction leave no doubt that abortion is infanticide. Bloody babies, beheaded babies, and dismembered babies lay in piles while we run about attending our busy little schedules, looking the other way.

Those we elect to serve our best interests do no better. They speak out of both sides of their mouths. Kansas Governor Kathleen Sebelius is a case in point. She said:

"My Catholic faith teaches me that life is sacred."
(Topeka Capital Journal, 2006)

However, she also said:
"I think for me and a lot of other people there are certain inalienable rights established for a person, but those are not applied in utero." *(Wichita Eagle, 1989)*

Since Sebelius made one statement in 1989 and the other statement in 2006, which statement is true? According to her documented actions, Sebelius remains a staunch supporter of abortion:

- She vetoed the bill to establish standards and inspections for the abortion industry - *twice.*

- In 2006, she was dubbed "*The best politician that blood money can buy!*" by an antiabortionist activist.

Sebelius is exemplary. Many of our elected representatives hold her views. The tragedy is when we dishonor one life; we dishonor all life - making judgments about whose life is worth living. We sink into a Third Reich mentality.

This is why it is okay for the abortion clinics to be filthy, disarrayed, infection-breeding laboratories. The lives of those choosing abortion don't matter either.

This is why 24 babies with spina bifida died in Oklahoma. This is why seven states loaned their foster children for pseudoscience to maim and kill. This is why the African-American men died at Tuskegee.

Only elitist judgments, personal agendas, political power are primary. *Nothing* else matters!

I (we) must confront the gross misrepresentations and outright fabrications that some are using to justify future abuses against thousands of those whose "quality of life" has been called into question. (Gibbs, 2006)

The story continues unabated . . . . .

The family asked the doctor about using hospice. The doctor said, "The patient isn't in pain and he isn't anxious. He doesn't need hospice. You should love him, company him, and support him. He doesn't have a terminal illness.

He is time-worn and his heart is weak, but he may die *later* rather than sooner. Personally, I don't recommend hospice because I don't agree with their views or their procedures."

Some of the family members pushed to employ hospice anyway, giving permission for them to give Ativan to the patient for *anxiety.* The patient died a few days later.

Even though hospice and their affiliates deny life-death

issues throughout the industry, the Hospice Patients Alliance receives ongoing complaints from hospice users. *(Hospice Patients Alliance)*

Ativan and morphine seem to be hospice's choice 'euthanasia tools.' Both drugs are routinely given in hospitals and hospice settings either singly or in combination.

Cautions regarding the administration of either of these drugs to the elderly are vigorously stated, warning they may depress the respiratory system resulting in respiratory failure, hypoxic cardiac arrest, and death.

Medicinal warnings also express the need for readily available resuscitative equipment for breathing support when administering these drugs to elderly patients.

Ativan and morphine have many identical side-effects, especially in the elderly. The most common are respiratory depression, confusion, hallucinations, and agitation. Giving the drugs together increases the likelihood of complications. Other side-effects include low blood pressure, low white blood cell count, seizures, and other psychotic symptoms.

The Hospice Patients Alliance again reports that: "One common method of hospice style euthanasia is to sedate the patient into a medically-induced coma, letting the patient die of dehydration.

Jay was taking both morphine and Ativan for his condition. While on the drugs, he was agitated, suffered sleep apnea, and had breathing problems. They were drugging him into oblivion.

After Jay repeatedly received both drugs simultaneously, his symptoms became worse. One day I noticed his struggle to breathe had worsened. I climbed into bed beside him, put my arms around him, and shook him every time he quit breathing.

When the medications wore off, I refused to allow the doctors to prescribe these drugs again. Jay's breathing returned to normal and he regained his mental capacity.

Jay had never suffered from sleep apnea before, however, the doctor ironically noted in Jay's records 'history of sleep apnea.'

Jay didn't receive Ativan again until Breech Medical Center administered the drug without my permission, side-stepping the "no-give medication warning" in his records.

Dead Silence

Truth is not only violated by falsehood; it may be equally outraged by silence. (Henri-Frederic Amiel)

'Desensitizing the people' are words used in Third Reich literature to describe the assault on the people. Massive propaganda techniques helped accomplish this goal.

When people continued to experience the new, brutal ideology in words and in actions, the initial gasps, protests, and rebuttals quickly become acceptance, compliance, and silence. The masses became silent. The churches became silent

Massive propaganda campaigns are hurled at Americans every day. Planned Parenthood kills and robs in the name of 'choice.' Big Medicine and Big Pharma kill and maim in the name of comfort care or quality of life. The ACLU continually rips at American heritage and American values in the name of personal equality. The list continues. The list is extensive.

Americans stand watching as prayer is banned from schools. We watch as thieves steal Christian holidays and morph them into neutrality. We watch people die in hospital corridors from lack of care.

We financially support and encourage abortion clinics as they kill our future Abraham Lincolns, Martin Luther Kings, and Jackie Kennedys. We watch Big Pharma and Big Medicine lie and rob and kill multi-thousands each year in the name of research and progress. We allow Hollywood to saturate us with filth and violence in the name of art and freedom of speech. America is anesthetized.

Americans continue to experience new ideology in words and in actions, our initial gasps, protests, and rebuttals have become acceptance, compliance, and silence. The masses are becoming silent. The churches are becoming silent. Only a few who demand accountability remain.

We mentioned watch-dog groups and committed individuals in the beginning of Part 4: The Third Reich in America. These dedicated tireless groups and individuals are working hard. They are sacrificing every day, facing the giants for all of us. But they can't do it alone. They need you and me. They need consensus, support, voice, and the collective power.

Catholic churches still have voice. They are on the internet; they provide information. They inform. They warn. Many are instructing their parishioners to "ask what is in it, before you take the latest vaccine" lest you receive baby parts. But too many others are silent.

Have we adopted blind-eye and deaf-ear philosophies? Have we abandoned the message and the mission? Are we falling before false kings, accepting their ideology, their actions, and their new reality?

America is on the slipper-slide of apathy and detachment. America is quickly forfeiting personal responsibility, critical thinking and evaluative analysis. America is becoming ripe for the take-over! When we awake from our *"political and spiritual slumbers"*, it may be too late.

"So obvious these moral lessons seem now, and so gross the malfeasance, that it seems redundant to revisit them. Certainly we do not need to study such gross moral pathology that could never happen again.

That is a dangerous conclusion. Moral lessons are quickly forgotten. Medical ethics is more fragile than we think. Moral reasoning based on defective premises tends to recur in new settings." (Leo Alexander Essays)

Part 4:

Wake Up and Die Right

Separating the Issues

You never change things by fighting the existing reality. To change something, build a new model that makes the existing model obsolete. (Richard Buckminster Fuller)

Dr. Peeno appeared on NBCs *Oprah Winfrey Show* on September 26, 2007. She said the American healthcare situation is almost the same as when she testified before Congress in 1996. The only difference is *"It is worse!"*

Michael Moore, maker of *Sicko, a* documentary on American healthcare, was also a guest on the show. Since Moore advocates for socialized medicine, the discussion leaned toward adopting socialized medicine in America. Participants on the show encouraged Americans to change the name socialized to something more palatable because of the negative response to that term in this country.

Remember one of the messages in this book? America changes the names of unsuccessful, mediocre, failed, and sometimes horrific histories, programs, or projects to help us tolerate the same behavior or results under a new name. This maneuver is meant to shelter us from the reality of our situation. It doesn't work. In truth, socialized medicine is for socialized countries. American is not one of them.

The first thing we must do is separate the issues. Do we want socialized medicine (basically a more entrenched form of America's current medical system, where the bureaucrats and elitists make the medical decisions and the consumers are out of the loop) or do we want a free enterprise medical system?

America is still creative. America is still ingenious. We have the mental, physical, product resources to create something new. We have always been the trailblazers, the mavericks, and the innovators. Why would we stop now? Why would we emulate someone else's system that doesn't work any better than what we have? Why would we want more of the same?

According to the information in this book, we must take the following actions to return American to state-of-the-art healthcare.

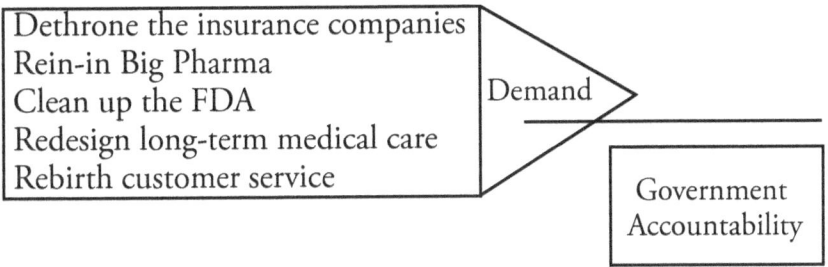

Dethrone the insurance companies
Rein-in Big Pharma
Clean up the FDA
Redesign long-term medical care
Rebirth customer service

Demand

Government Accountability

Facing the Insurance Lockdown
The limitation on personal freedom is a central defect of the American health care system. (Moffit and Marshall, 2006)

America's health insurance is bolted down in laws, rules, regulation, and policy. This includes federal and state tax policies, federal and state regulations, and benefit mandates. Therefore, in America's current healthcare system the government already determines the what's and how's in the individual's healthcare coverage.

"Among the 50 states, insurance providers are subject to at least 1,824 mandates for medical services, treatments, procedures and providers. *(Marshner, 2007)*

This over-regulated dilemma in addition to the incestuous relationship among the Big Medicinal four and the pressures constantly applied by special interest groups result in a highly politicized healthcare system.

"Healthcare finance delivery is largely politicized and driven by narrow but intense special interests, not by the free market or the personal preferences of individuals and families." *(Moffit and Marshall, 2006)*

In addition to these restraints, Americans must receive their health insurance coverage through employers. This is risky business for the consumer. The set-up gives the individual no choices in coverage and leaves him naked if he loses his job. The employers own the insurance policies.

Big Government provides tax breaks if an employee buys the employer-based insurance. If the individual chooses a plan of his choice, he must pay for the plan with after-tax dollars. This process contributes directly to the insurance monopoly. When there are no other options, a monopoly ensues.

Breaking the Lockdown Chains

Congress and the Bush Administration have initiated positive moves in the right direction. One of these initiatives is the tax-free high-deductible health savings accounts (HSAs). This is a beginning, but more is needed.

Many believe values based insurance would dethrone the giant healthcare conglomerates, provide options and voice for the consumer, and ensure medical coverage for all Americans.

Dr. Robert E. Moffit and Jennifer A. Marshall wrote: *Patients' Freedom of Conscience: The Case for Values-Driven Health Plans* which is available on the Heritage Foundation website at www. heritage.org. Following are some of the elements in Moffit and Marshall's proposal:

Personal Choice

Sponsorships of healthcare plans would include professional associations, employee organizations, unions, and faith-based entities.

Americans would be free to choose the plan most suitable to their needs. President George W. Bush also recommended faith based organizations and membership association insurance providers.

Moffit and Marshall pointed out that "Individuals and families could then secure coverage through plans that are compatible with their ethical or moral values." Many of these organizational and faith-based providers might include consumer boards to ensure consumer- oriented regulations.

Widen the health insurance options

Americans should have the option to buy insurance nationwide. America has interstate commerce, allowing us to buy anywhere in the nation. Interstate insurance would allow consumers to purchase insurance policies anywhere in the country.

States would retain their respective Insurance Commissioners who would monitor all insurances operating within the state. Insurance policies could be offered by the Catholic church, the Southern Baptist church, the Methodist church, athletic associations, credit unions, and academic institutions. The faith-based and association based possibilities are endless.

Provide Tax Equity

Individuals and groups must be free to purchase health insurance outside the workplace without facing tax code discrimination. Tax credits should be given to both the individual and the employer.

The refundable healthcare tax credit given to individuals would allow them to purchase insurance of their choice.

The employers' "defined contribution" to the employee's insurance policy also would be tax free. *(Marshner, 2007)*

The consumer should 'own' his policy. According to Moffit and Marshall, in a 'health insurance exchange,' the employee would designate his or her health insurance choice and the employer would contribute a specified amount to that insurance. Health care plans would *compete for the consumers' business.*

According to Moffit and Marshall, the independent tax credits should be:

> ➢ *Generous*
> ➢ *Refundable*
> ➢ *Universally available*
> ➢ *Vary according to the individual healthcare needs*
> ➢ *Variable dollar amounts increasing as family income decreases, providing greater assistance*

Moffit and Marshall also said all healthcare plans should be included as potential providers for Medicare, Medicaid, and the

State Children's Health Insurance Programs.

They contend that moving to a "national, consumer-driven health insurance" market would accomplish the following:

✓ *Create diversified customer-focused healthcare options*

✓ *Increase competition among the healthcare plans*

✓ *Decrease administrative costs*

✓ *Reduce health expenditures as younger enrollees with tax credits buy into the plans*

✓ *Provide incentives for insurers to write long-term healthcare contracts to retain customer base*

✓ *Stabilize prices due to diversification, long-term contracts, and focus on customer satisfaction*

✓ *"Revolutionize" customer service*

Moffit and Marshall wrote: "In 2005, the plan run by the Sisters of the Third Order of Saint Francis entered the Federal Employees Health Benefits Program. As noted, the Order of Saint Francis Healthcare System is a values-driven plan, governed by a Catholic perspective on health care." Similar plans could be -- and should be -- emerging daily.

Everyone in America would have access to health insurance. The values-based insurance framework is similar to the current children's state health insurance plans throughout the country. The families' payments for insurance premiums are based on income. When there is no income or it is under a given amount, the children qualify for Medicaid, the government healthcare coverage for the poor.

Values-Based Insurance Visually Portrayed:

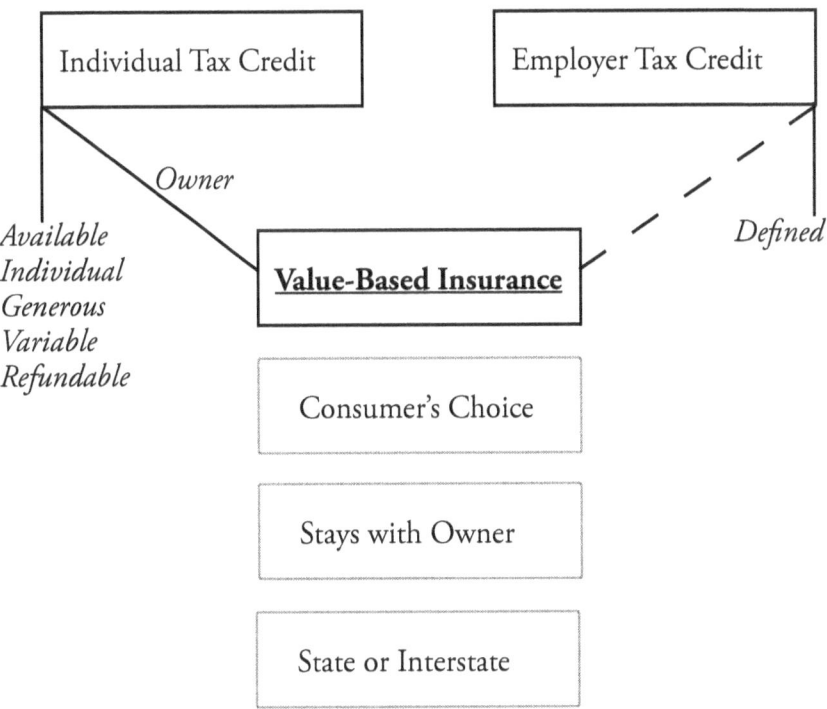

(Moffit and Marshall)

Consumer Responsibilities

The first thing every citizen must do is check their legislators' financial dependence upon the American healthcare industry. If the legislator is in financial bondage to the industry, healthcare reform through this representative will be a battle.

Vow to vote this representative out of office in the next election and let him know your intentions.

Next, move on to any legislator whose records demonstrate he is still capable of autonomous action. Call him. Write him. Hound him. Stay with him until he understands America wants values-based insurance. Stress the need for customer-based healthcare that honors the doctor/patient medical decisions.

Every citizen must stand up to their healthcare professionals. If he, too, has been purchased by insurance or another member of the Big Medicinal Four, find another doctor.

Inform the doctor of the decision to leave his practice and the reason why. Repeated negotiation to receive the customer service that we deserve without question is unnecessary. We must quit asking for service and demand it!

If insurance is the road-block to service, if insurance will not allow other physician choices, call the insurance company, complain to your legislator, call the insurance commissioner!

Personalities vary. Some confront easily. Others do not. However, every family has members who will confront. Elicit their help, but confront nonetheless. Unless we make our voices heard, we will be forced to endure what is handed to us.

Look around. Compare insurance policies. Choose the one with the most options. Choosing an HMO may not be the best choice. Even though it may seem like it is less 'out of pocket' money now, beware of the hidden snags.

We must make a statement, saying we want our voices back, we want service, and we refuse to allow our healthcare to compete with executive salaries and bottom-line profits!

If all else fails, prepare a mass email. Send it to every congressman and senator. This may be frustrating at first. I emailed every Kansas congressperson asking them to refuse to mandate the Gardasil vaccine in our state. I emailed over one hundred-twenty representatives and I received seven responses!

Before the mass email, I had emailed the representative from my district. I didn't receive a response. So I decided to email the entire Congress. To my regret, I still did not receive a response from my representative the second time around!

However, we all know this story would probably have had a different ending if the legislators had received 50,000 emails rather than one.

Rein-in Big Pharma

And remember, where you have a concentration of power in a few hands, all too frequently men with the mentality of gangsters get control. History has proven that. All power corrupts; absolute power corrupts absolutely. (John Dalberg-Acton)

America has an industry that is out-of-control. This industry is killing the American people for a dollar - billions of them. The industry has bought many of our doctors, our hospitals, and our legislators. Too many of them won't protect us anymore. It is time, America, to take the matter into our own hands.

Reining-in Big Pharma is a multifaceted task. We must expose the lies, demand transparency, halt the advertising blitz, and break the money-bond among the Big Medicinal Four!

Exposing the Lies
When material information is withheld, the message becomes a lie.

Think about it America! Protecting proprietary information of *'economic value'* does not mean economic value to you - the consumer. It means in the pocket money for Big Pharma and uninformed consent for America!

It is illegal for car salesmen to have proprietary information of economic value; selling cars they know have faulty brakes. If we learn that the salesman did this, we have avenues for recourse. Yet, the industry with our health in their hands may hide pertinent information that affects our very lives!

Protecting information for proprietary reasons of '*economic value*' is not okay! Americans should have been informed that Vioxx would significantly increase their chances for heart attacks. Americans should have been informed that Bextra would significantly increase their chances for kidney failure. And American women should have been informed that HRT Therapy would increase their chances for heart attacks, blood clots, and Alzheimer Disease?

Make calls to your legislators. Tell them we need to address the hidden information issues:

> ➢ Hidden information affects America's health and welfare! No information should be withheld for proprietary reasons of economic value - *ever*!

> ➢ Americans have the right to all information regarding their medications, the studies, the risks, the unknowns. We must know the best, cheapest, most benign drug on the market. We deserve to know when a naturopathic approach would be even better.

> ➢ America must initiate legislation prohibiting proprietary information of economic value! This legislation should be in place regardless of who researches, makes, or processes medications for the people.

Find legislators who are free from Big Pharma constraints, America. Tell them we must have an authentic, dedicated, brilliant, medical research department apart from Big Pharma, apart from Big Medicine, free to innovate, investigate, and create without money as the object.

Tell them to pay the medical researchers well, honor team work, encourage an interchange of ideas among the elite medical universities in the country. Give them a new FDA. Come on, America, we are leaders, we are innovators, we are pioneers. We can do better than this!

Demand Transparency
Transparency provides see-through access, leaving no corner,
no cranny to hide dishonesty, corruption, and deceit, ensuring
accountability, honesty, compliance, and customer-friendly
growth.

Big Pharma is a bully who violates anyone or anything in its
money-gobbling way. Big Pharma has secrets -- many secrets. The
secrets should be aired for all of American to see. Please ponder
the following information:

Our heads were turned, focusing on stem-cell research as Big
Pharma continued to experiment with aborted babies.

The National Institute of Health has funded AIDS research
involving baby organ transplants into mice. The idea, the
plan was to keep the experiments quiet, hidden. Big Pharma
and Big Government didn't want to suffer another backlash
from the public.

In the late 1990s, the public learned that Big Pharma
was involved in aborted baby "trafficking." They were using
aborted babies to develop polio, hepatitis A, chicken pox and
rubella vaccines. (Whitehead, 2006, Rutherford Institute)

"Fetal-tissue research: Making the best of a bad situation,
or sliding further down the slippery slope? Congress and the
Clinton administration's lifting of the fetal-tissue research
ban has turned human-remains trafficking into big business."
(World Magazine)

". . . .this country has been quietly producing vaccines for
the past 20 to 30 years from aborted fetuses. More shock:
that we have unknowingly vaccinated our children using this
"tainted source," a more polite way of saying we have used
pharmaceutical products from murdered babies. And utterly
outrageous is this: There is currently no other source available
for three widely used vaccines, namely, hepatitis-A, chicken
pox and rubella/MMR." (Catholic Exchange)

"Not only are babies, even at or near birth, being killed every day in America, this bastion of human rights, but their organs are also being harvested and sold on the black market. They are being dissected, sometimes while still alive, and sold piece by piece. Ears sell for $75 a pair, arms and legs $150, a brain for $999, tax not included. That's right; it's called the "unholy harvest." (Michael Savage, NewsMax.com)

Yes, it is illegal to buy and sell fetal tissue in the United States. However, those involved in the process have devised ways. "Fetal tissue brokers know how to deceive couriers so that a package of dead babies ships more easily than a carton of cigarettes." (Celeste McGovern, Focus On the Family)

The sale of fetal tissue is illegal, yet the FDA allows them in our drugs?

To reiterate a thought presented earlier in this book: *"The risk of vaccinating our children with vaccines containing DNA are many. "In addition to assessing the possibility of contamination of cell substrates with infectious virus, it is important to consider other agents . . . viral vaccines are developed and manufactured in cell substrates that may be derived from humans, and all human cells represent a finite possibility of being derived from individuals with a propensity to develop sporadic or familial Creutzfeldt-Jakob disease (CJD)." (Lifetalk)*

There are abundant resources available, describing the unholy harvest, baby-part trafficking, in America. In fact, there is so much information; it is amazing that anyone could miss it?

I just chose a scant few of these resources to report; the Rutherford Institute, World Magazine, Catholic Exchange, NewsMax.com, Focus on the Family, and Lifetalk. There is so much more. The information is out there, but we are sitting quietly in our chairs or dozing on our couches?

Wake up, America. This practice may touch your family in horrible ways. It may haunt your family. It may result in the greatest catastrophe America has ever known. We don't know. They don't know. No one knows.

Enlighten yourself fellow consumer. Ask your doctor what is in the pill, the salve, the vaccine. If he doesn't know, you *must* know. Do the research yourself and document the ingredients. Don't take it unless you know what is in it!

Halt the Advertising Blitz
Dismiss the hype; look at it with clear eyes.

Drug advertising is a recent phenomenon. The FDA legalized drug advertising in late 1997. *(Adams, 2007)*

The *Annals of Family Medicine* featured an article, *Direct to Consumer Advertising: Is it too Late to Manage the Risks,* written by Dr. David Kessler, former commissioner of FDA, and Douglas Levy.

In this article, Kessler and Levy reported, "Pharmaceutical spending on television commercials nearly doubled from $654 million in 2001 to a staggering $1.19 billion in 2005." Drug ads were legalized after Kessler left his FDA position and he contended that FDA should never have permitted television advertising. The United States is the only industrialized nation in the world to allow drug ads on television. *(Adams, 2007)*

When America just listens to Big Pharma's medicinal hype, we are harmed. The words tend to make us *think sick!* "Our own opinion about the state of our health is a better predictor than physical symptoms and objective factors such as extensive exams and laboratory tests, or behaviors such as cigarette smoking," said Dr. Larry Dossey, author of *Healing Beyond the Body.*

According to Dr. Dossey, this statement is substantiated by a work that was published in 1991. Ellen L. Idler of Rutgers University and Stanislav Karl of the Department of Epidemiology and Public Health at Yale Medical School conducted a study on 'health perceptions and survival.'

The study subjects were "twenty-eight hundred men and women aged sixty-five and older." And even more profound, the results of this study also mirrored results of five other large studies involving twenty-three thousand people ages nineteen to ninety-four. The results of all studies pointed to people as the best predictors of their own health.

"People who smoked were twice as likely to die over the next twelve years as people who did not, whereas those who said their health was 'poor' were seven times more likely to die than those who said their health was 'excellent,'" Dr. Dossey wrote.

Think of the difference it would make if America thought healthy rather than sickly! Think of the difference $1.19 billion saved on advertising costs each year could do for consumer prescription prices. Maybe Jay's five-day supply of Temodar wouldn't have cost $3,000.

American citizens must campaign to halt the advertising blitz. We must push for legislators to ban pharmaceutical advertising from the airwaves. In the meantime, we need the personal courage to shut it off! Cut the personal strings of dependency, America, become strong in the broken places, and say NO! Every time a pharmaceutical commercial airs, I mute the television. It is a refreshing, healthy thing to do.

Break the Money-Bond Among the Big Medicinal Four
Big money changes everything, focus, intent, goals, discrimination, and ingrained principles. That's just the way it is.

Our general practitioners were once our confidants. The people we could trust to give us our options, discuss the variables, and help us make wise choices.

Today, we listen to a foreigner, an alien to our lives, our families, our needs, and our dreams. We give our children untried, unproven concoctions in their veins to protect against maladies that may never happen. We take their recreational drugs to stiffen the anatomy and injections to plump our faces. We have forsaken exercise, nutrition, rest, meditation, relaxation, for the thrill of a pill. America, read on, it's all in our own hands.

The first step in reining-in Big Pharma is for America to get smart. Check out your personal physician. Whose side is he on? Ask the following questions and post the answers:

1. Does he offer a prescription at every visit?

2. Does he have a pharmaceutical plaque on his wall?

3. Is he is committed to patients or the drugs he can give?

4. Does he believe in nutrition and exercise?

5. Does he brag about the latest drug on the market?

6. If the patient develops an allergy, does he try another drug in the same category?

7. Does he hand the patient a drug pamphlet or does he sit and visit awhile?

America, know who your doctor is. Once the questions are answered, once you are satisfied you have the best doctor, build a relationship.

Tell him that you don't want to take "me-too" drugs. Tell him you don't want the "new-kid-on-the-block." You want the tried and tested drugs for your condition. These will be the cheaper, safer drugs.

Since I have always been a maverick, since I have always questioned the question, I had the following conversation with my doctor years before Jay became sick:

"I don't want to take this pill for my high blood pressure." I said.

"Why?" the doctor asked.

"I don't want to take it because one possible side-effect is anemia. I play tennis. I can go on the tennis court and have a stroke from high blood pressure, or I can go on the tennis court and have a stroke from anemia caused by this pill. Neither sounds okay to me."

"All medications have side-effects," he said.

"Yes," I answered. "But it is your job to find the safest drug for my condition. I want the drug with the least, most benign side-effects. I don't want the new kid-on-the-block.

I want the most tried and proven drug in your arsenal and I want the lowest dose possible."

The doctor prescribed two medications that had been on the market for years at very low doses.

That was ten years ago. I have not changed medications or doses since that day.

It is the patient's right to receive the best care possible, but we must be smart consumers. If we listen to Big Pharma hype on television, we are playing their game. They know the game. We don't. They have a plan. We don't. They don't care. We do. This information tells us they will always win!

These are simple things to do. Make sure your doctor is patient focused. Don't ask for the drugs advertised on television. Refuse me-too drugs. Take only tried and proven drugs for your condition. Then move on to the more difficult, confrontational activities.

One person's email may not shake the lawmakers. We must unite our voices. If one-hundred twenty representatives or senators received only fifty-thousand emails each, it might wake them from their slumber.

Becoming Strong in the Broken Places
Strengths comes from having – been there!

In his book, *No Excuses*, Kyle Maynard described the independent, healthy, self-protective attitude that I am advocating this way: "To live with 'No Excuses' means to take a robust, rugged individualistic attitude toward life's problems; it's about freedom and responsibility; it's about hard work and hard choices; it's about self-reliance that is joined naturally with family, friends, community, and faith. No excuses is about America as it used to be and should always be."

Let's become that America again. Let's make the decision to exert our free country prerogatives. Let's get up off the couch and demand honesty, customer service, and voice now!

Clean Up the FDA

The number of people killed by FDA-approved pharmaceuticals since 9/11 is equivalent to dropping a nuclear bomb on a major U.S. city. International terrorists could not even hope to cause the number of casualties in the United States that have been achieved by the drug companies working in conspiracy *with the FDA. (Mike Adams, 2007)*

Review the material. Big Pharma and Big Government are partners. We must separate them. We must make them accountable. The partnership is vile, it is corrupt. Big Government has some cleaning up to do. . . . .

The FDA

The FDA is at the top of the list. Its purpose is to protect. Its purpose is to ensure safety. Its purpose is to serve the American people!

A priority question to ask Big Government is: The Unholy Harvest, baby-part trafficking, is illegal so - how – by what means – does the FDA have the authority to sanction the use of these illegal cells in our drugs? It doesn't matter where these baby cells originate, America, China, Great Britain; harvesting them is illegal in this country and it holds great propensity for devastating harm!

The violations continue . . . . .

Dr. David Graham, FDA whistleblower, estimated Vioxx killed over 60,000 people in this country with the FDA's blessing.

The FDA approves prescription drugs that injure over two million of our neighbors, family, and friends and kills 100,000 each year.

After two years of investigation, I am convinced that the FDA's dependence on drug industry fees has created a deadly, unethical alliance and caused a principal-agent, pro-drug industry shift that puts millions of innocent Americans at risk.

In my opinion, due to its dependence on drug industry fees, the FDA's actions related to prescription drugs are suspect, and the Agency can no longer be trusted to act in its traditional capacity as a legitimate, objective, consumer protection agency." (Gary W. Lawson, DPA, 2005, doctoral thesis)

The FDA is a useless government bureaucracy that is costing Americans financially, medically, emotionally, and morally. Dr. Richard Horton, the editor of the British journal *The Lancet*, labeled the FDA "a servant of industry".

Americans must scream to their legislators, "Wipe the Slate Clean! Form a new FDA!" We must badger, hound, call, initiate complete legislative 'overhauls' and continue this offensive barrage, without pause, until someone hears us and begins the job. The FDA condition is not okay. It is urgent. It is an emergency. There must be change NOW!

Redesign Long-Term Medical Care

Palliative care focuses on symptom control and supportive care early in a patient's illness and is designed to both improve the quality of life for patients while they fight their disease and potentially increase life expectancy.

Palliative care is a new movement within the healthcare system. Palliative care provides all services that hospice provides. The one huge difference between the services is the family is in charge with palliative care.

In addition to helping the patient and his family satisfy their physical, intellectual, emotional, and spiritual needs, palliative care is the vehicle for information access and ensuring patient autonomy. Personal choice is an ultimate goal of palliative care.

Hospice *replaces* curative care. Palliative care *complements* curative medical care. Patients aren't tied-into dying within six months with palliative care!

After one full year of fighting the fight, struggling with numerous oncologists, neurologists, and dozens of other medical personnel, one oncologist finally decided to tell us that palliative care was a viable option.

If we had been working with this service from the beginning of Jay's illness, this book might not have been necessary.

Remember how I begged doctors for a conference? Remember how I wanted to brainstorm for the best treatment; remember my struggle to give Jay every possible chance for life? This finally happened three hundred sixty-five days later through the palliative care team. What a crime. They had been there in the wings throughout this whole devastating process.

The first thing the palliative care team did was initiate a meeting with the entire family. The team's doctor, nurse, and social worker met with the family to learn what the family needed and expected. This is when and where we set up the 'rules' for Jay's care.

The road still was not easy because palliative care is fighting a huge battle in today's death-oriented medical system. In our case, the palliative care team was sandwiched between health care pushing for death and family pushing for life.

The palliative care doctor became our spokeswoman, mediator, and confronter. She is the one who took on the battles, and she had many! The hospital quit giving Jay his thyroid medications twice. The palliative care doctor intervened. The nurses wouldn't keep Jay's bed elevated to thirty degrees. The palliative care doctor intervened. I continued to beg for nutritional supplements for Jay. The palliative care doctor intervened. Finally, in the last two months of Jay's life, the palliative doctor consulted with the nutritional specialist.

Ironically, Jay was receiving vitamins and minerals intravenously when he died!

The palliative care doctor called oncologists at both Kansas University School of Medicine and Duke University School of Medicine in search for answers. An oncologist at Duke University agreed to accept Jay when he could make the flight. However, they wanted Jay off the respirator before they would accept him.

After our experience, I believe that a member of a palliative care team should be present every time a doctor gives the news of a terminal illness. This team would provide the family with needed, valuable information, supporting their wishes and their world views. Their presence would automatically trump the hospital and doctor's institutional and personal views.

However, palliative care does have one problem in providing services - money. Unless they serve *with* hospice, they may have very little or no funds.

Hospice was a thorn in our sides. Their focus was death. Staff attacked me, my beliefs, and my determination. Palliative care saved me from illness and collapse.

Government agencies know government's pet-peeve. It is called duplication of services. Government is always searching for agencies that provide the same services so they can eliminate one.

Hospice and palliative care are duplication of services. Palliative care provides *every* service that hospice provides and more! Everyone who is served by hospice can be served by palliative care. However the reverse is not true. Since palliative care has services to fit every need, they should receive the funding!

When American families face the medical problems that Jay and I faced, whether it is cancer or some other devastating disease, they should ask for the palliative care team. Beware, some places will tell you hospice and palliative care are the same.

That is not true. Their focus, their care, their attitudes are different. Believe me. I know. I've been there!

Americans can eliminate hospice just for the asking - asking specifically for palliative care.

Home Health 'Monkey Business'

Government should rename Home health, calling it 'home-watch' because that is all home health regulations allow. Experts try to cram their years of specialty training into worried, tired, emotionally depleted care-takers' minds in a few short hours. (Silliman, 2007)

No family should experience what our family experienced- deciding between two thousand dollars for four quarts of salt water or $3000 for a five day supply of chemotherapy.

The choice was insane. If the doctor had been correct about Jay's need for IV fluids, either decision I made would have been fatal. We were not poor, but this expense would certainly put our finances in jeopardy, and many Americans couldn't have paid for the first $500.

We had nurses, a bath attendant, and rehabilitation therapists coming to our home. They were always in a rush and had very limited time with Jay regardless of his needs.

Their job was to instruct. My job was to perform!

One day I shared my concerns with Jay's rehabilitation therapist:

"I love working with my husband. I love doing puzzle with him, walking with him, exercising with him and reading with him. If you worked-out with him daily, I would still do all these things. It would be so nice if you would relate to Jay, work with him, and expertly rehabilitate him. It would be a relief for me to know that Jay was in the hands of experts a few hours a week!"

"I know." she said. "But we can't."

At the time, I didn't think the doctor's negative talk had fazed me. However, looking back, I must have believed the doctors on some level. I must have anticipated Jay's death as I know he did. Otherwise, I would have said goodbye to home health and bought our 'pleasure' wheelchair van one year earlier, when Jay first used the wheelchair.

When I think of the money Medicare paid home health for Jay's care, I am mortified. It is such a massive waste to the consumer, to the taxpayers, to the families. It is a joke. It is a travesty. Every time I relive it, I see the elitist on Capitol Hill making rules that have no practicality, no humanity, no sense. It reminds me of the common expression government workers often share:

"If it makes sense, we don't do it!

I honestly believe that every home health policy-making meeting should include consumer focus groups on the committee. More and more people are doing what Jay and I did: Leaving home health out of the equation, grabbing our own resources, and living until we die.

Specialists in Excess

We have a multi-billion dollar industry that is killing people, right and left, just for financial gain. Their idea of research is to see whether two doses of this poison is better than three doses of that poison." (Glen Warner, M.D. oncologist)

Medical specialists in America are running rampant. The result is the doctor dissects the patient right on his hospital bed. You have read the list of specialists who came to Jay's hospital room: oncologists, radiologists, neurologists, endocrinologists, infectious disease specialists, pulmonary specialists, skin specialists, gastrointestinal specialists.

The truth is the oncologist thought Jay was a glioblastoma. The neurologists thought Jay was a brain. The infectious disease doctors thought Jay was staph infection and the list goes on and on. Jay was not a person! He was only his parts!

According to an article by Dr. Dale Newton and Dr. Martha Grayson for JAMA, primary care physician numbers have steadily decreased since 1987. They gave several reasons for this decrease.

These reasons follow:

✓ *An increase in nurse practitioners and physician assistants in the office setting*

✓ *Decrease in career satisfaction of primary care physicians*

✓ *Declining income*

✓ *The widening reimbursement between sub-specialists and primary care physicians*

Many tout JAMA's fourth reason as the top incentive for physicians entering into the specialty field.

America needs medical specialists and we need the freedom to access them easily. However, when the specialists follow a national protocol for treatment, refuse to refer patients to elite research hospitals, and forfeit the doctor/patient relationship, they are somewhat like "jets" passing through the patients' rooms, making their decisions and care inferior to that of the primary care physician.

"Increasing the supply of medical specialists has resulted in a costly and unnecessary increase in demand for services." *(Santilli)*

The Final Analyses

No one in Government should ever think that the citizens they work for can't and won't scrutinize their actions. (Roy Barnes)

The problems are many. The problems are complex. American needs to place healthcare in a state of emergency and begin action steps today:

<u>Small Personal Steps to Recovery</u>
Know your doctor's relationship with Big Pharma
Expose his income from Big Pharma
Know if your doctor is involved in gain-sharing
Mute the television on drug ads
Ask what's in it before you take it
Refuse me-too drugs
Refuse the "new-kid-on-the-block" drugs
Consult the PDR at your local library often
Question, confront, self-advocate
Don't sign a living will. Designate health surrogate(s)

<u>Scrutinize your Legislators</u>
Check out your legislators financial income sources
Demand your legislator serve the people
Confront him/her on America's healthcare problems

<u>Call your legislators for:</u>

Values-Based Insurance
Increase reimbursement for primary care physicians
New FDA
Independent Medical Research Agency
Palliative care
Relaxed home health rules

The list is long. However, when we reclaim our autonomy, our values, and our collective voice, we will have state-of-the-art healthcare by the people and for the people!

Epilogue

The huge Medicinal Four is a tyrannical dynasty within America's midst. It is the darnel in our healthcare system, breeching order, meaning, and customer service initiatives. It rules with iron-clad alibis, substantiated by purchased politicians, physicians, and insurance executives. This colossus force ambushes the weak and vulnerable without remorse or regret. But remember . . . . those greater than this have fallen into nothingness!

If the task of cleaning up the system seems too monumental, consider this analogy.

> *"It is easy, really, to topple a large building, a corrupt system, or anything, even if it stands steadfast. This is what we must do. Circle the foundation, checking to see what makes it stand? Look for cracks, decay, and mortar crumbles.*
>
> *Then begin to pick at the weakest point, taking a rock or two, a corner embrace, or a weight-bearing pillar from an indiscreet place. The structure will creak, sway more violently in the wind, and become increasingly vulnerable to the next jab at its stance. That's all it takes to make rubble out of the powerful, the stout, the threatening . . . just that."*

So let's ponder what we must do, America. Where is the weakest link? If we push for Values-Based Insurance, breaking one monopoly down, so many other issues will already be addressed:

- ✓ Seeing the doctor we want to see
- ✓ Making personal healthcare choices
- ✓ Becoming top priority for our doctors
- ✓ Deciding our best insurance coverage
- ✓ Pushing Big Pharma to the outer edges
- ✓ Providing medical insurance to the masses
- ✓ Breaking the Medicinal Four stronghold, weakening the foundation

We must share our goals with everyone, telling friends and legislators, clergy, attorneys, neighbors, presidential hopefuls and the media for sure. We need to stand up and become strong in the broken places, forming advocate groups and information dissemination efficiency tools.

Once we have values-based insurance with interstate accessibility and have established ownership of our own medical policies, we will find other allies we didn't know we had.

Many doctors groups already shun the Big Pharma and FDA handholding tactics. If we own our insurance policies and our doctors are in the loop, calling the medical shots, once again, we can tame Big Pharma through ignoring their hype and ordering what is best for us at the time.

Now we have established a starting place. We have mapped out the steps. All we have left to do is stand up, join all our voices into ONE, and without hesitation reinstate state-of-the-art healthcare in our nation!

Bibliography

Abramson M.D., John. Overdo$ed America. New York, New York: Harper, 2005.

"Abortion Doctor Loses Medical License On Account of "Vile, Disgusting Clinic, Allegations of Cannibalism". LifeSite. http://www.lifesite.net/1dn/2005/jun/05061412.html. (17 May 2007)

"Abortion Hurts Women: Part 1: massive collection research. Physicians for Life. http://www.physiciansforlife.org/ content/view/1235/26/. (04 may 2005)

Adams, Mike. "FDA Censorship, Suppression of its Own Scientists". NewsTarget.com. Sunday, February 27, 2005. http:// newstarget.com/005032.html. (01 Jan 2007)

AFSCME in the Public Service. "*The Problems with Managed Care*". http://afscme.org/publicatins/3041.dvm. (28 Nov 2006)

"A List of Major Physical Sequelae Related to Abortion. Elliot Institute. http://www.afterabortion.info/physical.html. (10 Mar 2006)

Angell M.D., Marcia. The Truth About Drug Companies. New York, New York: Random House, 2004.

"Baby Parts Trafficing". Life Dynamics. http://www.life Dynamics.com/ (20 December 2006)

Barr, Christopher C. "Sleight of Handling: More Merck Magic Trick with HPV Vaccine. November 4, 20007. Cursador. http://healthtruthrevealed.com. (27 Mar 2006)

Bartlett, Donald L. and James B. Steele. <u>Critical Condition</u>. New York: Random House, 2006.

Black, Edwin. <u>War Against the Weak</u>. New York, New York: Four Walls Eight Windows, 2003.

Bren, Linda. "Cervical Cancer Screening". U.S. Food and Drug Administration. http://www.fda.gove/fdac/features/2004/104 _cancer.html. (23 August 2007)

Bright, Bill. <u>The Journey Home</u>. Nashville, Tennessee: Thomas Nelson, 2003.

Brody, H. "*The Faces of Syphilis*". http://www.msu.edu/ <u>course/hm/546/</u>tuskegee.htm. (13 Apr 2007)

"Call for Transparency, Accountability for NYC Foster Children AIDS Drug Trials". Wednesday, April 27, 2005. Alliance for Human Research Protection. http://www.ahrp.org/infomail/05/04/27.php. (29 October 2005)

Cauchon, Dennis. "*FDA Advisors Tied to Industry*". <u>USA Today</u>. Sept. 25, 2000.

"Congressional Records: U.S. Senate and House Records". http://www.senate.gov/page/layout/legislative/g_three_sections_ With_teasers/legislative_home.htm. (06 Mar 2007)

Dorsey M.D., Larry. <u>Healing Beyond the Body</u>. Place: publisher, 2001.

Gibbs, David with Bob DeMoss. <u>Fighting for Dear Life</u>. Minneapolis, Minnesota, 2006.

Gibbs, Nancy and Amanda Bower. "*What Doctors Hate About Hospitals*". <u>Time</u>. May, 2006, pp. 45, 47-49.

Grant, George, Grand Illusions, The Legacy of Planned Parenthood. Nashville, Tennessee, Cumberland House Publishing, 2000.

Greiber, Katherine. The Big Fix. Place: US Public Affairs, 2003.

Green, Tanya. "The Negro Project: Margaret Sanger's Eugenic Plan for Black America". Concerned Women for America. http://www.cuifa.org/articlesdisplay.asp?id=life1466& Department=cwa&categoryid=life. (20 June 2006)

Griffiths, Katherine. "The Interview: David Graham, FDA Whistleblower. February 12, 2005. http://www.findarticles.com/ (15 December 2006)

Groopman M.D., Jerome. How Doctors Think. Boston, Massachusetts: Houghton Mifflin, 2007.

Groopman M.D., Jerome. Anatomy of Hope. New York: Random House, 2005.

Godrej, Dinyer. "The Great Health Grab". New Internationaists. http://www.newint.org/issue362/keynote.htm. (14 Feb 2007)

"Guinea Pig Kids". Alliance for Human Research Protection. Tuesday, November 30, 2004.http://www.ahp.org/ infomail/04/11/30.php. (19 Mar 2007)

"Guinea Pig Kids: Vulnerable NYC Foster Children Forced to Test AIDS Drugs". New York Post, http://www.ahrp.org/ infomail/04/02/29.php. BBC News: http://news.bbc.co.uk/go/pr/ fr/-/1/hi/programmes/this_world/4035345.stm. (19 Mar 2007)

Harris, Steven M. "Proceed Carefully with Gain-Sharing Deals". Amednews.com. Newspaper for Americas Physicians. April 4, 2005. http://www.ama.asa.org/amednews/2005/ (20 October 2005)

Heimann, Jean M. "Late-term Abortionist George Tiller's Governor Kathleen Sebelius". Catholic Fire. October 23, 2006. http://www.catholicfire.blogspot.com/2006/

"How Big Pharma Secretly Bribes US Doctors with Billions of Dollars Each Year". Organic Comsumers Association. http://www.organicconsumers.org/articles/article_6364.cfm. (05 Jan 2006).

"In Hospital Deaths From Medical Errors at 195,000 per Year". American Iatrogenic Association. http://www.health. Groups.yahoo.com/group/iatrogenic/message/1451. (19 Mar 2007)

Kessler M.D., David, andDouglas Levy, J.D. "Direct to Consumer Advertising: Is it too Late to Manage the Risks?" University of California, San Francisco, California. http://www. Aunfamned.org/. (19 Mar 2007)

Kimel, Alexander. Holocaust Survivor. "Hitler's Popularity. On-line-Holocaust Magazine. http://www.kimel. Net/popularity.html. (07 December 2005)

"Kuru Disease". Wikipedia Encyclopedia Online. http://en. Wikipedia.org/wiki/kuru_%28disease%29. (15 March 2007)

La Puma, M.D., John. "Advance Directives in Managed Care: Are They Inspired by Love or Money?". Managed Care Magazine. http://www.managedcaremag.com. (22 Aug 2007)

Lawson DPA, Gary W. "Impact of User Fees (Drug Industry Money) on Changes within the FDA". May 2005 Doctoral Thesis. http://www.fdastudy.com/ (17 October 2007)

Lifton, Robert Jay. The Nazi Doctors. Printed in United States of America: Basic Books, 2000.

Loudon, Manette. "The FDA Exposed: An Interview with Dr. David Graham, the Vioxx Whisleblower". NewsTarget.com. Tuesday, August 30, 2005. http://www.newstarget.com/011401. html. (10 May 2007)

Lutzer, Erwin W. Hitler's Cross. Chicago: Moody Press, 1995.

"Mad Cow Disease". Healthy Americans. http://healthy Americans.org/topics/index.php?TopicID=24. (23 August 2007)

Maynard, Kyle. No Excuses. Washington D.C. Regnery Press, 2005.

"Medical Journals on the Dangers of Vaccines". Health and Beyond. http://www.chetday.com'novaarticles.heml. (06 September 2006)

McGovern, Celeste. "Canadian Researchers Named in Report on Baby Parts Market". August 23, 1999. Lifesite. http://www.lifesite.net/idn/1999/aug/990818a.html. (6 Apr 2007)

McGovern, Celeste. "The Sale of Baby Parts is Big Business in America – Unholy Harvest". Today's Family News. http://www.fotf.ca/ca/tfn/life/articles/unholy_harvest.htm. (16 Aug 2006)

"Medical Malpractice HMO/Manage Care". Sheller, P.C. Law Firm. http://www.sheller.com/practice.asp?PracticeID=58. (09 Mar 2007)

Moffit Ph.D., Robert. "Comparable Worth for Doctors: A Severe Case of Government Malpractice". The Heritage Foundation. http://www.heritage.org/research/healthcare/BG855. cfm. (23 Mar 2006)

Moffit Ph.D, Robert E. and Jennifer A. Marshall. "Patients' Freedom of Conscience: The Case for Values-Driven Health Plans". The Heritage Foundation. http://www.heritae.org/research/healthcare/bg1933.cfm. (28 Nov 2006)

Montague, Peter. "Perscription Drugs Kill: Another Kind of Drug Problem". Consumer Law Page. http://consumerlawpage. Com/article/drugs_that_kill.shtml. (10 May 2006).

Newman, Brandi. "Doctors of the Holocaust". http://www. remember.org/imangine/doctors.html. (27 Nov 2006)

Newton M.D., Dale and Martha S. Grayson M. D. "Trends in Career Choice by US Medical Students". JAMA 2003;290:1179 -1182. HHP://jama.ama.assn.org/cgil/content/full/290/1179. (6 Apr 2007)

"Pap Smear: Screening Test for Cervical Cancer". Women's Health. http://www.mayoclinic.com/health/pap-smear/HQo1177. (23 August 2007)

"Patient Focused Approach to Care". Private Physician Services. http://www.privatephysicianservices.com/patient_focus. php. (27 September 2006)

Peeno, Dr., Linda. "Managed Care Ethics". Testimony Prepared for U.S. House of Representatives. May 30, 1996. http:// www.thenationalcoalition.org/DrPeenotestimony.html. (20 December 2005)

"Prions: On the Trail of Killer Proteins". Learn.Genetics – Genetic Science Learning Center. The University of Utah. http:// learn. genetics.utah/edu/feature/prions/. (10 Mar 2006)

Reardon, Ph.D., David C. "A Post-Abortion Review: Abortion is Four Times Deadlier than Childbirth. Elliot Institute. http://www.afterabortion.info/PAR/V8/n2/finland.html. (13 Apr 2006)

Sharpe Dr., Robert. "The Scientific Case Against Animal Experiments". http://aerzte_gegen_tierversuche.de/conten t/en/resources/case_against_animal_research (27 Nov 2006)

Sherwood, Carlton. "Mathimatical Formula Decides Life and Death. Baby Doe: The Politics of Death. The Washington Times. July 10.1984. http://www.profiles.nlm.nih.gov/ (08 mar 2006)

"Sodium Borate Poisioning". Health Guide. New York Times. November 4, 2007. http//health.nytimes.com/health/guides /poison/sodium-borate-poisoning/overview.html. (04 November 2007)

"Stoned by Drugs". Vitality. October, 2002. http://www. Kospublishing.coml/htm/drugs.html. (22 Nov 2006)

Strode, Tom. "Reports of Trade in Fetal Body Parts Fuel Call for Congressional Hearings". Baptist Press. November 15, 1999. http://www.bpnews.net/prinerfriendly.asp?id-2631. (13 Feb 2006)

Tady, Megan. "Tracking Pharma Gifts to Doctors". The American Prospect. August 9, 2007. http://www.prospect.org/ Cs/article=tracking_pharma_gifts_to_doctors. (10 Jul 2006)

"Texas Governor Orders STD Vaccine for All Girls". MSN Health and Fitness. Associated Press. Saturday, February 3, 2007. http://www.msnbe.msn.com/ (16 June 2007)

"The Baby Parts Industry – Grim Harvest. Covenant News. http://www.covenantnews.com/babyparts.htm. (10 July 2006)

"The Hippocratic Oath". Edited Guide Entry. http://www. bbc.co.uk/dna/h2y2/a1103798. (15 August 2007)

"The Practice of Euthanasia and Physician Assisted Suicide in the United States". JAMA. http://www.jama.ama.assn.org/cgi/ Content/abstract/280/6/507. (30 October 2005)

"The Sterilization of America: A Cautionary History". Center for Individual Freedom. http://www.cfif.org/ (15 July 2006)

"The Truth About Margaret Sanger". Learn. http://www. Blackgenocide.org/sanger05.html. (17 May 2007)

"Three Girls Died, Others Hospitalized After HPV Vaccine". July 4, 2007. Big Pharma (Ceutical) Exposed. http:// Pharma.worldwidewarning.net/ (01 November 2007)

Whitehead, John W. "Aborted Babies are Big Business". The Rutherford Institute. Jan, 23, 2006. http://www.rutherford.org/ Articles.dbl/commentary.,asp:record_id=385. (13 Apr 2007)

Whitney, M. T. "Prescription Drug Deaths Skyrocket 68 Percent Over Five Years as America Swallows More Pills". NewsTarget.com. February, 22, 2007. http://www.newstarget.com/ 2021365.html. (20 December 2005)